TAYLOR MADE

TAYLOR MADE

CAR BUYING TIPS TO SAVE YOU **TIME** AND **MONEY**

STEVE TAYLOR

LIONCREST
PUBLISHING

TAYLOR MADE

Car Buying Tips to Save You Time and Money

ISBN   978-1-5445-1864-0 *Hardcover*

978-1-5445-1863-3 *Paperback*

978-1-5445-1862-6 *Ebook*

To my dad, Steve Taylor Sr., who taught me that the only place success comes before work is in the dictionary. Without his guidance and tutelage throughout the years, I would not be the man I am today. From him I inherited my passion for the car business and my focus on taking care of the customer. As Dad always says, "We're not in the car business. We are in the people business. Take care of the people!"

CONTENTS

FOREWORD

The very first time I received an email from Steve, I could tell he was different.

Here he was, the owner of a car dealership, telling me he was driven by two things: to be different from the competition and to stand out by being a fun place for his employees to work.

I was intrigued. I learned more about the crazy marketing stunts he attempted with his dealerships.

I heard about the giveaways: the bobbleheads, chia pets, and two-dollar bills. I heard about his crazy ads featuring a Bill Clinton impersonator and about how he stayed on his roof until a certain number of cars sold.

He definitely thought differently, but what about his team? Did they share his unique thinking style? Did they have fun at work?

I had to meet Steve and his team and see it first-hand.

When I arrived in Toledo, I was blown away. I was welcomed with open arms and treated like I was part of the Taylor family.

At dinner my first night in town, I was inspired by how hungry he and his team were to learn about delivering a better experience. It wasn't about how to sell more cars. It was about how to take care of people, with the focus on making customers feel better about their car-buying experience.

I believe you can tell a lot from a business by the happiness levels of the employees. I spent two days speaking and connecting with his team. They were engaged the entire time and brought more energy than I've seen from a group of colleagues. They were laughing and sharing ideas. It was obvious how much they cared.

When you think about car dealerships, the word "caring" isn't usually the first word that comes to mind.

This wasn't by accident. It was intentional, and it started at the top.

Steve Taylor is different. This book, *Taylor Made*, is different. A car dealer sharing everything about the industry is different. From how to get a better deal, to how to negotiate, and how to have a better experience.

This is the blueprint on how to eliminate stress and anxiety when buying a car. In *Taylor Made*, Steve puts his customers first. In the car industry, that's different and practically unheard of.

Buying a car should be fun. It should be exciting. You shouldn't walk up to the lot, dreading the experience. You should be informed and prepared.

All you need is this book.

I wasn't expecting to learn as much as I did about the entire car buying experience.

Going the extra mile is what Steve Taylor and Taylor Automotive are all about.

His life motto is, "Be a difference maker and try to make a positive difference in someone's life every single day." He is hungry to make a difference. For his team, his customers, and his community, and it shows.

He cares. He is a lifelong learner. He's not your typical car salesperson. He's a friend and a family man.

In *Taylor Made*, he brings you into the family.

This is a book about transparency, authenticity, and how you make people feel.

We can all learn from Steve and his dealerships, whether we're buying cars or building relationships.

Steve is different. Taylor Automotive is different. This book makes a difference.

Read. Take notes. Take action.

You'll be better off because of it.

JESSE COLE
OWNER, SAVANNAH BANANAS
AUTHOR, *FIND YOUR YELLOW TUX*

INTRODUCTION

Phil and Regina walk into a car dealership and instantly feel the sharks swimming around them.

Merle, a middle-aged salesman with bad teeth and a greasy combover, meanders up, cigarette in hand.

"Help you?" Merle asks, sizing up his next victims in a way that seems anything but helpful.

"Well, I hope so," Phil responds. "We're looking for a safe, reliable car for my wife. Something fuel efficient. We're leaning toward a used four-door sedan."

Merle nods as he blows smoke out the corner of his mouth. "How much you wanna spend?"

"We want our payments to be as low as possible," says Regina. "Paying three hundred dollars a month or less would be ideal."

"Well, I've got just what you're looking for! Gotta keep the little lady happy, right?" he says as he elbows Phil and winks at Regina.

Merle abruptly turns and walks toward the exit. Phil looks at Regina and shrugs. "I guess we're following him," he whispers as they both turn and walk out the door.

Outside, Merle strolls past a few rows of used four-door sedans and stops in front of a brand-new $50,000 SUV. He looks back at Phil and Regina with a wide grin and points his cigarette hand toward the vehicle. "Nice car, huh?"

"Uh, it's a nice car," Phil replies, "but that's not what we're looking for."

"Oh, come on. Let's take this beauty for a spin. You'll love it!"

"No, really. I'm sure this is out of our budget. What would the monthly payments be?"

"Oh, we could make it work. Definitely get you down to four hundred or five hundred dollars a month."

"What?!" Phil asks, trying to control his frustration. "That's not what we said. Maybe we could go back and look at some of the sedans we passed. Those might be closer to our price range."

While Phil was talking, Merle opened the driver's door, and he's now waving Regina toward the front seat. "This car has all the bells and whistles! And it will keep the little lady safe. Come on, honey, let's take it for a drive."

Phil's jaw tightens. "As I told you, this is not what we're looking for."

But Merle is already walking toward the building. "Just sit tight. I'll be right back with the keys."

Regina looks at Phil and says, "Let's go. I'm not giving this guy our business."

"I'm with you. Let's try the other place on Main Street."

IT DOESN'T HAVE TO BE THIS WAY

Although this is a fictional account, it's not too far from what some people have experienced or envision happening at a dealership. For many people, car buying is an agonizing, stressful ordeal. They worry about being ripped off. They don't feel prepared to negotiate. They don't know anyone in the car industry who can offer advice or tips, so they feel alone. In truth, many people would prefer jury duty or getting a root canal over going to a dealership to buy a car.

The good news is that car buying doesn't have to be this way! You can buy a car without being stressed out and without paying more than you want to. It's possible to find a dealership where the salespeople actually listen to you and help you find the best car for you.

How do I know this? Because I've been helping people buy cars with minimal stress for more than twenty years at my family's dealerships. I'm going to share what I've learned so you can choose a dealership that meets *your* needs and understand how to buy the car you want on your terms.

CARS ARE IN MY BLOOD

In the early 1900s, my mom's grandfather, Charles Fisher, and his older brother started the Fisher Body Company in Detroit, Michigan. Eventually all seven Fisher brothers worked for the company, which was the first to build the closed-body vehicle—even before Ford. From the 1920s through the 1970s, Fisher Body supplied closed bodies to General Motors for all of its vehicles, making over 40 million bodies during that time.

My dad's dad worked for General Motors at the Omaha plant in the late 1940s and was promoted to the Chevrolet division in Detroit soon after my father was born. My grandfather died when my dad was fourteen, and my dad started working at General Motors shortly after. My grandfather's friends got Dad an after-school and summer job in the mailroom.

After high school, Dad traveled to Cullman, Alabama, where he was supposed to attend seminary. However, he was in love with a girl back in Detroit—my mom—and he never finished. Instead, Dad attended Michigan State University and after graduation, he attended General Motors Institute (GMI) in Flint, Michigan After district manager stints for Chevrolet in Phoenix, Arizona, and Planview, Texas, my dad transferred to Toledo, Ohio, where I was born.

Dad worked for a local Chevrolet dealer and moved up quickly. The owners had my dad go check out another dealership that was up for sale. After Dad gathered all the information, he took it to the owners, and they decided they weren't interested in buying the dealership. But my dad was. He borrowed money, got a line of credit, and took out a loan. On August 1, 1979, at age thirty-two, my dad bought his first dealership: Taylor Buick in downtown Toledo.

I started "working" at my dad's dealership when I was around six years old. A couple Saturdays a month, I went into work with my dad and did little jobs around the dealership: I pulled weeds, polished brass, picked up cigarette butts, and swept the floors. When I got into junior high and high school, I washed cars, and during the summer I helped move cars and reseal the blacktop lot. One summer I even painted the whole dealership.

After college, I landed my first full-time job as a salesperson at our Buick/Isuzu dealership. I learned the ropes from the older salesmen, who didn't let me get away with sloppy work just because of my PhD (Papa Has a Dealership). One time after I didn't follow the right process, Bill Cassidy, an older salesman who had worked with my dad for years, told me, "I don't care whose kid you are. If you ever do that again, you won't be working here." I didn't do it again.

I sold cars for quite a while. In August 1998, I helped launch our newly acquired Kia franchise as one of the senior salesmen. We sold Kias on the used car lot connected to our Cadillac store in downtown Toledo.

Fast-forward to January 1, 2000. We opened a brand-new Cadillac dealership on the Central Avenue Strip, also known as Automobile Row. With the opening of that store, we no longer needed our satellite Cadillac store in the suburbs. We turned that store into Taylor Imports, where we sold Kia, Isuzu, and Daewoo. I started running Taylor Imports in early 2000. There were just four of us working at this store, and we struggled to sell cars, to put it mildly. We didn't even have our own finance person, porter, or receptionist on-site; they were all downtown at one of our other locations.

In 2001, we had an opportunity to lease an old Chinese restaurant building that had been converted into a used car lot. The building was closer to the rest of the dealerships on the Central Avenue Strip, but we were not *on* the strip. We had a gravel lot and an old building that definitely looked more like a Chinese restaurant than a dealership. Taylor Imports was sort of the laughingstock of the local car-selling world.

I talked to someone from an ad agency who shared a simple pitch he'd used with other Kia dealers. It asked three questions: "Do you have a job? Do you have a hundred and ninety-nine dollars? Do you want a new car?" They hired voice impersonators to do radio ads using voices such as Bill Clinton, Arnold Schwarzenegger, Austin Powers, Mike Tyson, and anyone else who was making the news headlines.

"We're killing it with Kia dealers across the country," the guy told me. "All I need from you is a commitment for a three-week radio buy at ten thousand dollars a week, and we'll make you one of the largest Kia dealers in the country."

I told him it sounded great. I saw this as an opportunity to do something different, to really pave my own way with the Taylor Imports dealership.

My dad didn't agree. "You're crazy," he told me. "That's thirty thousand dollars in advertising. You stick to your budget of two hundred dollars a car." We were selling about thirty cars a month, so our budget amounted to $4,500 for the same three-week period.

For seven months I kept going back to my dad with this idea, telling him we had to try something different. Finally, he agreed.

In our first spot, we used a Bill Clinton voice impersonator to introduce the all-new Kia Rio. It even included something about Monica Lewinski. It stood out. It was unlike anything anyone in our area had done.

And it worked. The first day we ran that spot, we had 117 phone calls from people like Phil and Regina who were hardworking, budget-conscious folks and needed a safe, reliable car. We had people take the bus to our store. We had people ride their bikes to our store. People responded to the simple questions. They showed up and said, "I have a hundred and ninety-nine dollars. I have a job. I want a car." We had maybe four or five salespeople working at Taylor Imports at that point, and we couldn't handle all the business. We had to hire our own finance manager, more salespeople, and someone to help us acquire used cars. From 2001 to 2002 we probably lost more business than we earned because we really didn't know what we were doing. But we started selling cars and never looked back.

As we grew, I started setting goals for our business: largest dealer in Toledo, number one Kia dealership in Ohio, largest Kia dealer in the Midwest region. We hit each of these goals, and we outgrew the old Chinese restaurant. In 2004, we acquired more land around the restaurant and built a brand-new facility. In 2005, we gave up Isuzu and Daewoo, moved into the new building, and became Taylor Kia Toledo.

Since then, Taylor Kia has received several awards and recognitions for sales and customer satisfaction. Every month, Kia recognizes the largest dealership in the United States, and we have earned that distinction many times. In 2009, we were awarded International Kia Dealership of the Year, and in 2019, we were named to the prestigious Kia President's Club for the eighth time. We now sell roughly ten thousand new and used cars per year.

All this to say, I know a little something about helping people buy cars.

HOW I CAN HELP

Growth like that takes more than car sales. It takes a certain culture. At our dealerships, we focus on building a community. Because our customers have a positive car-buying experience, they tell others and they come back when they need another car for themselves or their children.

My life motto is "Be a difference maker." I try to make a positive difference in someone's life every single day. By writing this book, I'm hoping to make a positive difference in your life by helping you enjoy a positive car-buying experience. This book will provide tips, answer questions, and give you actions to take before you even step on the lot. By being prepared up front, you can ask the right questions, know what to expect, minimize anxiety, and save yourself time and money.

Here's what you'll learn in the pages that follow:

- Insider information on how and why car dealerships use marketing. Having more realistic expectations regarding interest rates and monthly payments can help minimize stress and disappointment at the dealership.
- How to find a dealership that cares about more than just the bottom line. Spoiler alert: look for a dealership that is involved in the community, that values its customers, and that creates a positive culture for its employees.
- Financing options, the importance of good credit, and what you can do if your credit isn't the best.
- Tips related to buying or leasing new cars and used cars. These chapters will help you determine whether new or used is best for you.

- Negotiating tips and tricks. Being nice and respectful goes a long way when you're working with a car salesman—or anyone.
- The pros and cons of selling your used car on your own versus trading it in at the dealership when you buy a new or used car.
- The truth about ancillary products such as Extended Service Contracts (ESC) and Guaranteed Asset Protection (GAP) coverage, with stories from customers who have purchased them.

Are you looking to buy a car? Let me help you get a great deal and minimize stress. Who knows, you might actually enjoy your next car-buying experience!

CHAPTER 1

MARKETING 101

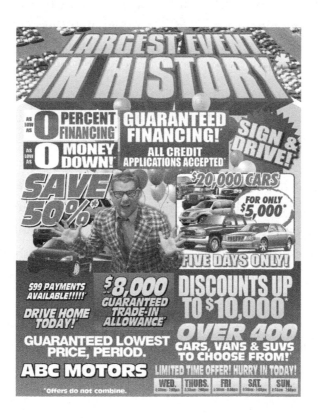

If you read a newspaper, listen to the radio, or watch TV, you've most likely seen or heard ads offering incredible deals like the one shown here. They dominate the airwaves and print of local papers. Perhaps one of these incredible offers has even drawn you into the dealership. When you arrived, however, you probably found out that you didn't get everything offered. In fact, you only got one discount (that's what "offers do not combine" means) and you didn't even get to choose which one was applied.

Why would car dealerships do this? Are they really out to scam potential buyers and anger them in the process?

Like any other business, car dealerships use marketing and ads to get your attention. They want you to call, click, or come in. Ultimately, they want to sell you their product—in this case, a car.

In this chapter, we'll discuss typical marketing strategies that car dealerships—and other businesses—use to draw you in and make a sale. If you understand up front what dealerships are doing and if you learn to read the fine print, you will be better prepared when you walk in to buy a car. With more realistic expectations, you are less likely to feel ripped off and more likely to have a stress-free car-buying experience.

MARKETING STRATEGIES

Why does any company advertise? To sell a product, first and foremost. Whether the business sells jewelry, cell phones, or beer, the goal is the same: stand out, be recognized, and draw people in to buy what they're selling.

If you've ever watched the Super Bowl, you've seen the commercials. You might even watch the game for the commercials. Companies are willing to spend millions of dollars for a thirty-second spot because they want you to remember them the next time you're shopping for _____ (fill in the blank). They want top-of-mind awareness that leads you to visit the website or buy the product.

Any great marketing campaign sells on an emotional level. Think of the Budweiser commercial with the Clydesdale touching noses with the adorable puppy. Or the 1980s Folgers coffee commercial where the son comes home at Christmas and surprises everyone. The family wakes up to the smell of fresh-brewed coffee and comes downstairs to find Peter is home. Companies know that people can be persuaded to make purchases based on emotions.

The automotive industry is one of the most crowded and competitive business segments in the world. Dealerships compete for the same small group of people who are in the market for a car at any given time. To grab the attention of those looking to buy, dealers need to stand out, so consumers say to themselves, "I need to go to *that* dealership!" The most effective way to do this is by appealing to buyers' emotions through cash back offers, discounts, and free prizes.

Car dealerships know that people want low car payments, and $199 is the sweet spot. Our old ad campaign capitalized on this number: "Do you have a job? Do you have $199? Do you want a new car?" People heard it and thought, "Oh my gosh. I do have $199 and a job! And would I like a new car? Heck yeah. You're telling me I can have one for $199? I better go check it out." People who weren't in the market for a new car were suddenly in the market.

As of mid-2019, the average monthly payment on a new car was $550, yet dealers across the country still advertise payments of $199. Why? That's the price people want to pay. (And if you find the right car, put enough money down, and have a high enough credit score, you really can pay only $199!)

If potential buyers read the fine print, they realize not everyone qualifies for the $199 special. But dealerships are counting on the fact that people will respond to the ad on emotion and come in. Dealerships are also hoping that once people are there, they will find a car they love at a price they can afford, even if it's not $199.

Buying a car is different than buying an appliance like a washing machine. No one gets excited about buying a new washing machine. People buy a washing machine because they need it—the old one broke or they moved into a new home that doesn't have one. Cars, on the other hand, elicit an emotional response. Americans have a love affair with the new car smell. They love the personality a new car gives them and the way it makes them stand out. Marketing appeals to these emotions.

In addition, marketing creates a need and then provides a solution, whether the product is a weight loss supplement or a new car.

For example, one of our commercials says, "Stop driving a car you hate." If you hear that message enough times while you're driving to work in a car you hate, you just might be persuaded to come in a buy a new car.

At any given time, only 2 percent of the population wakes up and says, "I need to buy a car today." In car dealership advertising, we're going after a bigger percentage of the population, more than the 2 percent who actually need a car. We're going after those who don't necessarily need it, but they're sick of driving the one they have or they have a big stain on their seat or they hear a new clunk in the engine.

THE FINE PRINT

I'll admit it. Some car dealership advertisements are confusing, and you have to read the fine print very carefully to find out if you and your purchase qualify (remember the ad at the beginning of this chapter?). Customers sometimes feel duped when they realize the $5,000 discount was for "select" models (e.g., the loaded-up $48,000 model), not the midrange $30,000 model they settled on. That car might only have a $2,000 incentive.

Some ads also seem to use a bait-and-switch technique to attract customers into the store and then sell them a more expensive car. Perhaps you've had this happen: a dealer advertises a discount on one particular model, but that model is no longer available when you arrive. Or you see an ad for payments at $199 a month, go into the dealership, and find that you can't qualify for those terms.

If the dealer never had the car in the first place, that qualifies as bait-and-switch, which is illegal. If the dealer had four cars at the advertised price and they sold on Saturday morning but the ad runs until Sunday, that might appear to be bait-and-switch but it's technically legal. Likewise, if you can't get the advertised monthly payment, it could be that you don't qualify based on your down payment or credit score. It doesn't (necessarily) mean the dealership is guilty of false advertising.

TAYLOR TIP

Always read the fine print. If the ad says the discount applies to "select cars," call and ask what cars qualify as "select." If the disclaimer says "with approved credit," understand that your credit score will probably have to be pretty high in order to qualify. You can save yourself a lot of time, headache, and disappointment if you know exactly what is being offered *before* you step onto the lot.

Not disclosing terms, false advertising, and bait-and-switch techniques are all illegal, and the attorney general in each state takes these practices seriously. Dealers have huge handbooks on advertising dos and don'ts. For example, disclaimers have to be typed in a certain size font and the qualifying terms (amount of down payment, length of loan, minimum credit score, etc.) have to be clearly spelled out.

The bottom line is that dealers, like every other business, are trying to sell their product. They use advertising to get customers to respond by calling, visiting the website, or driving to the dealership to take a look.

NOT ALWAYS TOO GOOD TO BE TRUE

People love the idea of getting something for nothing. This is why millions of people play the lottery and participate in the Publishers Clearing House sweepstakes. It's why Chick-fil-A has a VIP night when they open in a new town and people camp out in the parking lot. People want free stuff. Dealers understand this, and they market accordingly.

We ran a commercial that no dealer had ever done in our town: buy a Kia Sedona and get a Kia Rio at no additional cost. The Sedona was loaded up, so it was the most expensive model on the lot, and the Rio was a stick-shift base model: no air conditioning, no power locks, nothing extra. People were attracted to the idea of receiving something at no additional charge (we couldn't say the word *free* in our ad), and they saw the Rio as a go-to-work car that would get good gas mileage, or as a first car for their teenager.

People were skeptical about the Buy One, Get One offer because it sounded too good to be true. The local news even came out to interview me, possibly thinking they might blow the whistle on a shady deal. Once they found out it was legitimate and interviewed a customer who actually received the second car at no additional charge, they reported the truth in the news and it helped us even more.

Some dealers may be using emotions, creating a need, providing a solution, *and* giving you a really good deal at the same time. It doesn't have to be one or the other.

ALLY, NOT ENEMY

Why am I sharing these marketing secrets? I want to give you a more positive view of car dealerships before you go in to buy a car. Most dealerships and car salesmen are not out to get you. They are not trying to cheat you through false advertising. Car dealerships are simply using the same marketing techniques as every other business. Like Folgers, Budweiser, and innumerable other companies, dealerships play on your emotions, create a need, and provide a solution to get you to come in and buy their product.

If you see dealerships in a new light, you will be more likely to view salespeople as your ally in finding a new car. Without your defenses up, you might actually enjoy the whole experience.

One key factor is finding a dealership you trust, where you feel comfortable and at ease. The next chapter has tips for finding a dealership that cares about customer experience more than the bottom line.

CHAPTER 2

RESEARCH THE DEALERSHIP

"All right, here's how this is going to work," Dr. Short tells the high school seniors sitting in the audience. "We're going to draw ten names. If your name is called, you'll come up here, get a T-shirt, put it on, and choose an envelope. In that envelope is a prize."

The principal goes on to explain that the prize in three of the envelopes is a car key. One of those keys will start one of the three cars sitting onstage, and the student holding that key will go home as the owner of a brand-new Hyundai Elantra.

The PTA president turns the crank on the big brass drum. She pulls out a name and hands it to the principal. The auditorium falls silent. When the principal reads the name, the audience explodes and the student makes her way to the stage.

One by one, names are pulled and read. I'm standing onstage, and I shake hands with each senior as they walk past to line up. After all ten students are onstage, the principal counts to three, and the students open their envelopes. The seniors with the keys hold them up, and the other seven students return to their seats.

The student with key number 1 gets first pick of the cars, then number 2, and finally number 3. All three keys work on one of the cars. The question is who picks the right car.

Each student walks to their chosen car, opens the door, and sits behind the wheel.

"Put your keys in the ignition and I'll tell you when to turn," I say. "One, two, three!"

All three students turn their keys, and the audience cheers when one of the cars roars to life. I walk over and congratulate the student, who is smiling ear to ear.

Our car giveaway is one of my favorite days of the whole year. It marks the culmination of the Driven to Succeed program that Taylor Hyundai sponsors at Perrysburg High School in Perrysburg, Ohio.

The program rewards students who go above and beyond in academics, extracurricular activities, attendance, and behavior. For every achievement during their senior year—every A received, every club or sport participated in, having perfect attendance—students earn an entry into the raffle. Their name is written on a slip of paper and dropped into the hopper. Disciplinary action results in a name being removed.

Before we award the car, the seniors watch a video compilation of photos from their past twelve years in school, and then I talk about goal setting and achieving success in the next chapter of their lives. I love rewarding some lucky senior for all their hard work. It's a way to give them a little extra momentum heading into the next stage, whether it's college or the workforce.

The Driven to Succeed program is truly a community event. We've been sponsoring it since 2010, and now parents, teachers, students, and the local news know it's happening and look forward to it every year.

Community involvement like this is one thing to look for in a dealership you do business with. It shows they appreciate their customers and want to give back to the people who give to them through their business.

In this chapter, we'll discuss ways to identify a dealership that cares about community, as well as its customers and employees. This kind of dealership will strive to make your car-buying process as positive as possible because they want customers for life.

CUSTOMERS, COWORKERS, COMMUNITY

If you're in the market for a new or used car, you have many options: publicly traded dealership chains, independent used car lots, and more. How do you choose one over another?

We've found that return customers appreciate three main things about our Taylor Automotive dealerships: we value our customers and treat them like family, we create a positive culture for our coworkers, and we're involved in our community. Our customers like doing business with us because they feel comfortable. They can tell we're trying to create a relationship that lasts beyond the sale. We want them to come back for service as well as future car purchases.

If you consider the following tips and make a few dealership visits, you'll know when you find a place that you trust.

CUSTOMERS

When you're researching dealerships, one of the most important things to find out is how they treat their customers.

Buying a car is a huge deal. After a house, it's probably the largest purchase you will ever make. When making that kind of decision, you shouldn't feel pressured. You also shouldn't feel like a number or just another transaction. You should feel like you're part of the dealership family. You should feel confident that this dealership will take care of you for years to come, long after the sale is over.

The best way to find out how customers feel about their experience is to ask. Do you have friends and family who have bought a car from a local dealership? Ask them how it went:

- Did the salesperson listen to you?
- Did you feel pressured to buy?
- Did you get a fair price?
- How were you treated after the sale?
- Did the dealership follow up with you to make sure you were completely satisfied?
- Would you buy another car from that dealer?
- Would you take your car there for service?

Another way to research past customers' experience is to check the dealer's website and Facebook page, as well as

Yelp and Google, for customer ratings, reviews, and testimonials. Don't limit yourself to one source. Read several reviews, both positive and negative, from multiple sources.

As you read the reviews, keep a few things in mind:

- Dealerships can't make everyone happy. Some people leave poor reviews for things that are unrelated to the service received. If you see a few one-star reviews on a dealership, don't let that alone dissuade you.
- Dealerships' responses to reviews says a lot about their customer service. Did they get defensive and push back on the customer, or did they try to make it right? Sometimes customers leave an updated review based on the dealership's response, for example, "I went to this dealership and had this problem, but the manager contacted me and he completely turned my experience around. Now I'm a happy customer, and I'll recommend this dealership." Also look for dealerships' responses to five-star reviews. Do they thank customers for positive comments?
- Read (or watch, if they're videos) testimonials as well as reviews. You'll find testimonials on the dealership's website and Facebook page. In testimonials, people might highlight a particular salesperson who helped them have a positive buying experience or a finance manager who clearly laid out the payment options.
- Find testimonials for the service department as well as sales and finance. If you're buying a new car from this

dealership, you want to make sure they're going to take care of you after the sale, when you come back to have your car serviced.

- You can't believe everything you read. Unfortunately, people leave false reviews. They may exaggerate or completely lie about what happened. Some people leave reviews—positive and negative—when they've never visited the dealership. Additionally, some dealerships buy phony positive reviews. (For what it's worth, we see more fictitious and negative reviews on Yelp, whereas we receive mostly positive reviews on Google and Facebook.)

When people buy new cars and have those cars serviced at the dealership, they often receive satisfaction surveys afterward. While most dealers don't post scores from these surveys, they do publicize Customer Satisfaction Index awards won as a result. Those trophies or banners are often on display in the dealership or posted on their website.

If dealerships receive a certain number of 10 out of 10 or 5 out of 5 ratings, they can win various awards from the manufacturers. Look for those banners or awards at the dealership as well.

COWORKERS

The second element to research is the culture of a dealership, which includes the engagement and happiness of the employees.

As a potential buyer, why should you care whether employees like working at the dealership? There are several reasons:

1. Happy employees are more enjoyable to deal with. If you dread buying cars and you know you're probably going to do this more than once in your lifetime, wouldn't you rather work with someone who's pleasant and helpful?
2. Happy employees are probably treated well, which says a lot about how you'll be treated as a customer.
3. Happy employees are likely rewarded for their on-the-job efforts, which means they will be more motivated to work hard for you.
4. Happy employees tend to stay at their job longer, which means you have a known point of contact in the future.

Culture is an intangible quality. You know when you walk into a business that has a positive culture, and you know when you walk into one that doesn't, even if you can't put it into words. You can feel it.

To research the overall culture and engagement of employees, take a look at the dealer's Facebook page and other social media. Look at the events, announcements, photos, and comments. Also check out the About Us page of the dealership's website. Here are some specific things to look for:

- Are employees recognized for doing a good job? For example, we do a Weekly Wow to honor an employee who has gone above and beyond. We write a little summary of what the employee did, include a photo, and post it on the Taylor Automotive Facebook page. Other dealerships might post an Employee of the Week (or Month) award.
- Does it seem like a fun place to work? Does the dealership throw family picnics or holiday parties? We sometimes hold contests between stores and then take our money machine to the winning store. The employees who achieved the highest in the contest (whether it was sales or service) win a chance to go into the machine to grab cash. We also have the Taylor Games, which is seven weeks of competition that culminates in a track and field day with all eight stores, their families, and friends.
- Has the dealership received any Top Place to Work awards? Many cities award recognitions like this annually.

Some dealerships have reviews from employees about their experience working there. You can also check third-party websites such as Glassdoor and Indeed to see what current and former employees have to say. As with the customer reviews, read several comments, both positive and negative. Again, be aware that people may leave false reviews.

COMMUNITY

No matter where you live, you've probably seen Little League uniforms with car dealer logos across the front or signs at soccer fields or announcements that a city event was sponsored by a certain dealership. In general, dealerships want to support the community that supports them.

Our town holds parades to celebrate Fourth of July and Christmas. Perhaps your city does something similar. You may not have thought about this, but it costs money to pay for the floats, fireworks, Santa Claus, transportation for the band, police escorts, and more. Who pays for these things? Local businesses, including car dealerships.

Before you buy a car, start looking at how dealerships in your community give back (or don't). Especially take note of the areas that are important to you. Did a dealership sponsor an event at your child's school or fund the cancer walk you participated in?

Again, check the About Us section of the dealership's website, as well as their Facebook page and other social media accounts. That's where they might advertise information or post pictures related to community events they're sponsoring or causes they've supported. Some dealerships don't announce their participation, so you can also ask around to find out about a dealership's reputation and how involved they are in the community.

IN-PERSON VISIT

As a potential customer, don't limit your research to online reviews and testimonials. Make an in-person visit to each dealership you're considering and take a good look around. This is another way to get a feel for the dealership's culture and the attitude of its employees. Do the salespeople seem happy? Are you greeted with a smile and a handshake? Or is the only salesman in sight sitting in a corner with his feet on the desk reading the newspaper?

In addition, an in-person visit will tell you a lot about the level of service you can expect. A dealership that doesn't have time to wash the cars or clean the windows probably doesn't have time to give you an excellent customer experience.

PRESENTATION AND CLEANLINESS

You drive up to the dealership, park your car, and walk toward the showroom. What is your first impression?

- Does the dealership as a whole feel welcoming?

- Is there enough customer parking, and is it easy to find?
- Is the main entrance to the showroom clearly marked?
- Is the service department entrance clearly marked?
- Are the cars clean?
- Are the cars parked in an organized way?

As you walk toward the showroom, look at the grounds and the building exterior:

- Has the grass been mowed?
- Are the bushes watered and trimmed?
- Are there weeds pushing up through the cracks in the cement and in the planters?
- Are there cigarette butts on the lot and/or near the doors?
- Are the windows washed?

After you walk inside, look around for a second:

- Is there clutter on desks, up against the walls, or in other areas?
- Are the floors swept?
- Are there burnt-out light bulbs?

AMENITIES

While amenities aren't essential, they certainly contribute to a more pleasant car-buying experience:

- Does the dealership have free Wi-Fi?
- Does the dealership provide up-to-date magazines and newspapers?
- Does the dealership have fresh-baked cookies, popcorn, beverages, and other snacks?
- Does the dealership have a service department? (Some independent dealerships don't.)

TAYLOR TIP

When you visit a dealership, ask to speak to the general manager or sales manager. When you meet the person, say something like "I'm in the market for a new car, and I'm doing research to make sure this is a place where I want to do business."

I can almost guarantee the red carpet is going to be laid out for you. If the manager comes out of his office to greet a customer who has requested to see him, he is going to make sure the potential customer has a fantastic buying experience.

A TALE OF TWO RESTAURANTS

Let's say you have two options for dinner. Restaurant A is noisy and crowded. You walk up to the counter and place your order with a kid who's smacking his gum and scowling. Then you look for a table, but find they are either taken or covered with trash and leftover food. After your meal you head toward the door and walk right past an employee, who completely ignores you.

At Restaurant B, you walk up to the counter and the employee greets you with a genuine smile. When taking your order, the employee asks for your name and then thanks you by name after your transaction is complete. The dining room is free of trash and the tables are clean. When you're finished eating, an employee comes up and asks if she can take your trash. When you say thank you, she says with a smile, "My pleasure."

You get food in both places, but one provides a nicer, more comfortable customer experience. Likewise, you can buy a car at one of many dealerships, but some will provide extra care that lets you know you are more than a number. Dealerships like this are trying to establish a relationship. They want you to feel taken care of when you need service or another car in the future.

Finding the right dealership is as important as finding the right car. It may take more time up front to look for community involvement, to scope out the culture, and to find out what customers think, but it will be worth it in the long run.

After you find a place where you want to do business, it's time to think about your purchase. Before you get your heart set on a car, it's wise to find out what you can afford. In chapter 3, we'll talk about financing options, the importance of credit, and what that means for monthly payments.

FINANCING OPTIONS

When he's working with customers to figure out financing, one of our top sales professionals, Jerry Gerken, uses what he calls the Gerken Triangle (figure 3.1). The conversation usually goes something like this:

"OK, you've got the car you want," Jerry says, as he points to the tip of the triangle, "you've got the payment you want (points to one of the sides), and you've got your money down (points to the other side). You get to pick two of the three sides, and I'll guide you toward the third."

The customer usually nods, and then Jerry continues. "If you tell me you want this car and that payment, then I might tell you that you need to put eight thousand dollars down."

"What? We can't afford that!"

"Exactly. So, if you want zero money down and a payment of three hundred dollars a month, then I'm going to have to show you the car that works."

The Gerken Triangle
How I make car buying easy

How much do you want to spend on a *monthly payment?*

How much do you have or need for a *down payment?*

What's your *ideal vehicle?*

Figure 3.1. The Gerken Triangle

With this triangle, Jerry has simplified a complicated and intimidating process. He guides customers through the financing options and helps them find the best solution in terms of car, monthly payments, and money down.

Everyone needs a Jerry because there are so many factors involved in financing: your credit, the interest rate, the loan term, the money down, the purchase price, available rebates, dealer discounts, and more. (Having a salesman like Jerry in your corner is another reason to find a dealership you trust!)

Financing is often one of the most stressful parts of car buying. With the information and tips provided in this chapter, you can go into the dealership armed with knowledge that will save you time, money, and lots of headaches.

SO MANY FACTORS

Many people think financing is fairly straightforward. The dealership checks your credit score, determines the interest rate, and boom—you have a monthly payment based on the car price. Figure 3.2 shows that this is not the case.

Vehicle	2020 KIA Forte	2020 KIA Forte	2020 KIA Forte	2020 KIA Forte	2020 KIA Forte	2020 KIA Forte	2020 KIA Forte	2020 KIA Forte
MSRP	$20,398	$20,398	$20,398	$20,398	$20,398	$20,398	$20,398	$20,398
Lease or Finance	Lease	Lease	Finance	Finance	Finance	Finance	Finance	Finance
Money Down	$3,000 down	Zero down	Zero down	$3,000 down	Zero down	Zero down	Zero down	Negative (-$3,000)
Terms	36 months	36 months	84 months	60 months	72 months	60 months	60 months	60 months
	12,000 miles/year	12,000 miles/year	$1,250 rebate	$1,250 rebate	$1,250 rebate	no rebate	$1,250 rebate	$1,250 rebate
			12% APR	8% APR	10% APR	4.25% APR	8% APR	8% APR
Monthly Payment	$260	$360	$365	$385	$410	$429	$445	$505

Figure 3.2. This example shows eight different payment options for the same person with the same credit buying or leasing the same Kia Forte at the same price.

The factors affecting the final monthly payment include:

- lease versus buy
- amount of down payment
- interest rate
- rebate with higher interest rate
- no rebate with lower interest rate
- having a trade-in with negative equity (meaning you owe more than the car is worth) and
- variation in loan term

And figure 3.2 doesn't even show all of the options. For example, incentivized interest rates down to 0 percent are available, but typically not to someone with a credit score in the 600s as in this example (more on the importance of credit later in the chapter).

Notice that in general, the shorter the term, the higher the payment; the longer the term, the lower the payment. If you have a certain monthly payment in mind, you might not be able to reach it and stay in the term length you want. Given the example in figure 3.2, if you're buying the Kia and want to stay closer to $350 a month, you could bump up to a seven-year loan instead of five years (eighty-four months instead of sixty).

Each situation is different. Some people are rate conscious and want to get the lowest interest rate possible when buying a new car. Other people might pay off the car early, so they'd rather lower the original principal balance by taking the rebate and then shorten the term by paying it off early. Your salesperson can help you figure out which option is best for you, given your credit, budget, down payment, and car choice.

Another factor to consider: if you have a trade-in and you owe more than it's now worth, you have what's called negative equity. For example, if you still owe $10,000 on your car and the trade-in value is only $7,000, you have $3,000 in negative equity.

Most banks require you to pay off the existing loan (the negative equity) before they give you a new one. You usually have two choices: you can add the existing balance to the purchase price of the new car, or you can pay the balance up front. If you take the first option, you're basically rolling the negative equity into your new monthly payments. Using the numbers from the above scenario, that would mean you're financing $30,000 instead of the actual sales price of $27,000 because you had $3,000 in negative equity. If you pay off the old loan first, then you have to put down $3,000 up front, but your new loan will still be for the actual sales price of $27,000.

DEALERSHIPS AND FINANCING

You may have heard that dealerships make money on the financing side. That's true. But they don't make a dime unless they sell a car! That means it's in their best interest to hire managers who know how to structure deals to get customers approved. If customers get approved, they buy cars, and dealers make money.

The fact is, however, not everyone gets approved. Even if a manager sets up the deal just right, the bank can still deny the application based on the customer's credit history or low score. It's not as easy as wanting the car and writing up the paperwork.

Keep this in mind when you go into the dealership: salespeople and finance managers are on your side. They set up the paperwork with the goal of getting you approved, not denied. They want to fit a car payment into your budget so you can drive off in a new car.

Ideally, a dealership will educate you through the financing process. Like Jerry Gerken, a salesperson should help you understand which cars you can afford so you don't waste time and energy thinking you can get your dream car for $199 a month and no money down.

If the salesperson takes time to ask you questions before heading out to the lot, that's a good sign. If he or she doesn't, you take the initiative. Tell the salesperson what the car will be used for, what your budget is, whether you have a trade-in, and how much money you can use as a down payment. All of this information will help the salesperson know up front whether you can afford that $30,000 SUV or whether you're going to have to scale back a little. This will save you time and stress.

Don't be the person who goes into the dealership wanting to drive every car, finds out she can't afford any of them, and then complains about how long the process took. Do your homework ahead of time. Remember the Gerken Triangle, look up your credit score, and find out what you can truly afford.

WHY DOES CREDIT MATTER?

Financial institutions look at your credit score as an indication of your trustworthiness. In other words, can they trust you to pay if they loan you this money? Credit scores affect your ability to get approved for a loan in the first place.

I wish we could deliver a car to every customer we work with, but the reality is that banks won't finance everybody. We might work half a day with a customer, test-drive multiple cars, and finally settle on one that meets the customer's down payment and monthly budget. Then we sit down to structure the deal and send it to the banks, and we can't get the customer approved because their credit is so low. It's frustrating not only for the customer but also for the salesperson.

If you're denied a loan because of credit issues, don't take it out on the salesperson. They may have just spent half a day helping you, but if you don't get approved, they don't get paid.

When you do get approved, your credit score will determine your interest rate. Phil and Frank may be interested in buying the same car for the same price, and they may even make a similar down payment. Yet Phil could end up paying $200 more a month because he has lower credit and can only get approved for a high-interest rate loan.

BAD CREDIT

If you have bad credit, you likely know it and may even be embarrassed by it. You may have been turned down by several dealerships already because they don't have options (known as subprime loans) for those with low credit scores.

If you're in this boat, call a few dealerships before you go in. Be up front about your credit and ask if they have subprime financing options. Don't write yourself off just because you have bad credit. Many dealerships have subprime options for getting people with low credit approved.

If you can be approved through a subprime lender, that's a great way to re-establish your credit. You will probably have to settle for a less expensive car, and possibly a used model. You will also pay a higher interest rate, but this is short-term. If you can show that you consistently made on-time payments on a higher-interest loan for twenty-four to thirty-six months, you might be able to get out of that loan and into something with a lower interest rate. You might even be able to buy the car you originally wanted.

TAYLOR TIP

Most dealers now have an option on their website that allows you to apply for a loan online. If you've been turned down by another dealership, you might appreciate the opportunity to try again with a different dealership from the comfort of your own home. After submitting the application online, follow up with the dealership over the phone. Most dealers want you to come in because it's easier to work with someone face-to-face, but online is a good way to start the process.

Another option is to apply online through a bank or credit union or through a third-party auto loan website. If you do that, know that your information is being passed on to many dealers and you're probably going to receive multiple phone calls.

Credit Repair

If you have poor credit, you might also consider credit counseling to help raise your credit score. These pay-to-participate programs can help you re-establish yourself and raise your credit by sending letters to dispute certain bills, especially medical bills. They also have options for consolidating debt into a loan with a lower interest rate.

We had a customer with a low credit score who wanted to trade out of her old-style Sorento that had a lot of negative equity. As a result, the finance manager couldn't get her prime rates. The monthly payment we could get was too high, so she passed on the deal.

This finance manager went above and beyond to see if he could help the customer. He visited the TransUnion Dispute Center on her behalf and followed the proper steps. Within seven days, the customer's dispute was complete (this was unusual, as it normally takes two to four weeks).

When the finance manager checked the customer's score again, it was over 700. As a result, he was able to get her approved for an extended term on a new car. She was thrilled—so thrilled that she asked us to fix her husband's score as well, and he then bought a vehicle.

As you can see, fixing your credit score may not be as hard as you think. It could take months, depending on the severity of the issue, but it can be done. If you're in this boat, visit the TransUnion Dispute Center to see if you can fix outstanding balances or negative hits against your credit. There are no guarantees, but it's worth a shot.

Some of you may have arrived in your current situation through a series of unfortunate events. A husband gets laid off and then the family suddenly experiences expensive medical bills. A businesswoman with excellent credit has an unexpected tragedy and is unable to pay some bills. As a result, her credit drops from 700 to 550. It happens. If you're in this situation, consider the credit counseling mentioned earlier.

Some of you may have bad credit because of your spending habits. If that's the case, start living on a budget, and not just related to buying a new car. If your spending exceeds your monthly income, you're going to have credit problems. Learn to live within your means.

TAYLOR TIP

If you have bad credit, try to make a decent down payment on your next car. From a bank's perspective, someone who puts $3,000 down is less likely to stop making payments than someone who puts no money down. As a result, you're more likely to get approved even with a low score. The more money you put down, the better chance you have of getting approved if you have bad credit.

Buyer Beware!

Certain car lots and dealerships will try to take advantage of you and your bad credit situation. These "buy here, pay here" lots typically sell used, higher mileage cars in the $4,000 to $6,000 range. Sometimes they advertise 0 percent interest, but they've already raised the price to double what the car is actually worth. These dealers know people are desperate because they have bad credit and they've run out of options. We've seen people come in to buy a new car and trade in a vehicle they've bought at one of these lots. They might owe $6,000 on a car that's not worth $1,000.

Be careful when you're buying from a buy here, pay here lot. You don't want to get stuck in a junker that breaks down soon after you drive away. Instead of getting desperate and jumping at one of their options, take time to pay off debts and raise your credit. Then go to a reputable dealer and buy a car through proper financing channels.

GOOD CREDIT

Aside from getting approved more easily, good credit gives you more financing options. The higher your credit score, the more options you have. As you can see from figure 3.3,[1] good credit can help you secure a lower interest rate, but that's not the only benefit. You can also extend the length of your loan, choose to lease instead of buy, and qualify for special financing options.

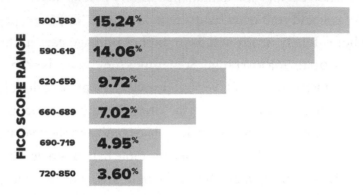

AVERAGE RATES BY FICO SCORE: 60-MONTH LOAN ON NEW CARS

FICO SCORE RANGE

Range	Rate
500-589	15.24%
590-619	14.06%
620-659	9.72%
660-689	7.02%
690-719	4.95%
720-850	3.60%

Figure 3.3. These figures from ValuePenguin.com show the importance of good credit when it comes to interest rates.

One option you might have with good credit is financing over the vehicle's MSRP (manufacturer's suggested retail price). That means you could finance your taxes and fees, as well as the purchase price, and not have to put any money down. In essence, the bank is saying, "You're fine. You don't need a down payment, and you can roll your taxes into the loan. Because you have such good credit, we'll loan you more money than that vehicle is worth."

What often prolongs the car-buying process is figuring out financing. If you have good credit and get approved immediately, the finance manager doesn't have to spend time structuring and restructuring the loan and calling multiple lenders trying to get you approved.

Financing your new car can be stressful. Do yourself a favor and learn your credit score before you start car shopping. You might be embarrassed if it's low, but it's better to be prepared so you know what to expect and what you can afford. It's also better to slow down and reestablish yourself rather than rush into a situation you might regret.

In the next chapter, we'll look at the benefits of buying a brand-new car over a used car, as well as factors to consider when you're deciding on make and model.

CHAPTER 4

NEW CARS

Every car buyer has a unique situation and story. Let's look at three examples; perhaps one of them is similar to your story.

A young couple came into the dealership to look at a car. Both had some bruises to their credit, and there wasn't a lot the salesman could do for them at the time because of their credit score and bank parameters. A few months later, the wife returned to the dealership and approached the same salesman. "My husband is such a great father," she said. "He's a great husband. I really want to help our family get this car. He's been through so much in his life."

"Well, let's see what we can do," the salesman replied.

The wife spent several hours with the salesman, trying to

find a car that would work given the family's financial limits. Finally, they succeeded: they found a brand-new car with several manufacturer rebates that brought down the price to something the family could afford. The wife bought the car, and the salesman drove it to the couple's house, where the husband was home watching the kids. The wife went into the house and brought her husband outside.

There, sitting in their driveway, was a brand-new Hyundai Elantra with a big red bow on top.

∗ ∗ ∗

A grandmother and granddaughter came into the dealership. They walked around for a bit, and then the grandmother said, "What do you think of this car?" It was a brand-new Kia Sportage SUV.

"Grandma, it's beautiful!" the granddaughter replied. "That's why I'm going to college, so one day I can have a car like this."

"I'm so proud of you," the grandmother said, as she handed her granddaughter the keys. "This is your car, to get you through college."

This granddaughter was the first person in the family to go to college. The salesman told me, "I don't know who cried more, the granddaughter or me."

* * *

A customer who had just gone through a bad divorce came into the dealership. Bills were piling up, and she had lost her car in the divorce settlement. We were running a promotion where the customer could buy a car and get a certain amount of cash back to pay off bills.

This woman heard about the deal and came in. She bought a car and received $6,000. With this money, she paid off her debt and turned her life around. "That car deal was the best thing that happened to me," she later told us. "When everything else was going wrong, you guys helped me get my financial situation back in order."

For many people, buying a new car is a life-changing experience. It represents new opportunities and possibilities. In this chapter, we'll walk through aspects of buying a new car so you can have that magic moment too, whether you buy that new car for yourself or a loved one.

WHY BUY NEW OVER USED

Americans have a fascination with new cars. They love the new car smell and the extension of their personality that a new car represents. When people buy a new car, they show it off to family, friends, and neighbors. People don't get as excited when they bring home a used car. It simply doesn't have the same appeal.

Some people don't like buying someone else's previously owned vehicle. They like knowing every single mile that's put on that car. They like knowing if it's been in any accidents, if the oil has been changed, and if the car has had its regularly scheduled maintenance checks. With a used car, you don't know what kind of off-road driving the previous owner did or what happened in the back seat.

In addition, new cars come with a warranty, which provides peace of mind. You know that if something goes wrong in the first three or five years, you can go back to the dealership and have it taken care of (more on warranties in chapter 8).

In some states, when you buy a new car and trade in a used car, you only pay sales tax on the difference. So, if you buy a $20,000 new car and trade in a $10,000 old car, you only pay tax on the difference: $10,000. This benefit doesn't apply if you trade in and buy a used car.

Finally, you can generally get lower interest rates on new cars compared to used.

FACTORS TO CONSIDER BEFORE YOU BUY

There are so many cars out there, and in many ways, they

are quite similar: they all have four wheels and a steering wheel. They are all made of sheet metal. They all have stereos. Why will you pick the one that you pick? What is important to you?

When our salespeople walk around the lot with customers, they ask questions to determine what is most important related to six areas contained in the acronym SPACED:

- Safety
- Performance
- Appearance
- Comfort
- Economy
- Dependability

As you consider what you want in a new car, use the SPACED acronym. (Use SPACED when shopping for a used car, too, which we'll cover in the next chapter.) How important are safety ratings? Would you rather have something sporty looking, or do you need to drive six or more kids to practice on a regular basis? Now is the time to think through these questions, before you're walking around the lot.

MANUFACTURER

Check out the manufacturer itself. If it's important that your car be manufactured in America, do some research to verify which vehicles are made in the United States. US manufacturers such as Ford and General Motors build some of their cars in Mexico, for example, while Kia (a Korean company) builds some of its cars in Georgia.

Some manufacturers support charitable causes, which might be a reason for you to buy from them. Hyundai, for example, has a charity called Hyundai Hope on Wheels. For every Hyundai sold, a certain dollar amount is donated to fight childhood cancer.

MPG RATING

If fuel economy is important to you and you're living on a tight budget, you'll want to research MPG (miles per gallon) ratings on the cars you're considering.

Websites such as Car Payment Calculator (https://www.carpaymentcalculator.net/calcs/gas-budget.php) can help you determine your expected annual fuel bill based on your estimated miles per year, the MPG of your car, and fuel price per gallon. Trucks and SUVs often get lower miles per gallon, whereas sedans are generally higher. The difference in your monthly fuel expense could be a hundred dollars or more.

Perhaps you currently drive a ten-year-old car, and you're worried that you can't afford a $300 monthly car payment for a new car. Consider this: by upgrading, you could get a car that gets significantly better gas mileage, saving you $80 a month in gas. In a sense, that car payment would really be $220 a month. See figure 4.1 for an illustration of how buying a new car could save you hundreds in gas.

TRADING IN YOUR VEHICLE COULD SAVE YOU HUNDREDS ON GAS EACH YEAR!

VEHICLE	CURRENT CAR	NEW CAR	SAVINGS
Current Cost per Gallon	$2.60	$2.60	
Miles per Year	15,000	15,000	
Avg MPG	18	32	
Monthly Est. Fuel Cost	$181	$102	$79
Annual Est. Fuel Cost	$2,167	$1,219	$948

Figure 4.1. Don't forget to consider MPG ratings when you're looking for a new car.

SAFETY RATINGS

If safety is a high priority, check out ratings on vehicles you're considering. The Insurance Institute for Highway

Safety (https://www.iihs.org/) provides crash test safety results, as does the National Highway Traffic Safety Administration (https://www.nhtsa.gov/).

WARRANTY

When you're shopping for your new car and comparing make/model, make sure you take manufacturer warranty into consideration.

The basic bumper-to-bumper warranty covers all the moving pieces of the car: window regulator, sideview mirror, radio, power locks, power seats, and so on. (Ironically, it doesn't cover the actual bumpers. That's simply the term used to describe the comprehensive coverage. It also doesn't cover normal wear-and-tear items such as batteries, light bulbs, and brake pads.) Typically, basic warranties are three years/36,000 miles, whichever comes first, but some manufacturers offer five years/60,000 miles.

The power train warranty covers everything under the hood: engine, transmission, trans axle, drive shaft, and so on. The power train warranty is typically five years/60,000 miles, but a few manufacturers offer ten years/100,000 miles.

If you buy a car that has a three-year/36,000-mile warranty and you plan on keeping the car for two or three years, then you probably won't care about having a longer warranty. However, if you plan on keeping your car for at least five years, you might consider buying from a manufacturer whose cars have a longer basic warranty.

MANUFACTURER REBATES

Manufacturer rebates started as a way to move cars off the lot. Customers were given hundreds or thousands of dollars for buying certain models that weren't selling well. Now the general public anticipates giant rebates, and manufacturers like Ford, General Motors, and Dodge continue to offer them.

Once you've determined what make and model you're looking for, search for the manufacturer rebates that might be applicable to you. This is yet another reason to do your research! Rebates change every month, so check dealer or manufacturer websites often. Manufacturers typically have several rebates going at any given time, some of which you'll qualify for and some of which you won't. If you're a member of the military or a recent college graduate, for example, you might qualify for a special rebate, in addition to the manufacturer's rebate available to everyone.

Another type of rebate is the competitive bonus rebate. This applies if you're buying a certain car and you owned a similar car in the past manufactured by a competitor. For example, if you're looking at buying a Kia Sorento SUV, and in the past you owned a model on the qualifying list (for example, a Honda CRV), you would qualify for an additional $500 off.

If you have negative equity on the car you're trading in, look for a new car with a manufacturer rebate. This will help offset some of the negative equity you're carrying over to your loan. If your trade-in has $5,000 in negative equity and you find a car with a $3,000 rebate, now you only have $2,000 to carry over to your new loan.

DEALER CASH

When dealers sell or lease certain models, some manufacturers offer additional incentives called *dealer cash*. These rebates are similar to customer cash back incentives, except that the dealer can choose how to use the money. Dealer cash is usually offered on select models from the manufacturer, and the models and amounts can change monthly.

Given the choice, most dealers prefer dealer cash over rebates on specific models because they can do what they want with dealer cash. They can use it to pay salespeople a bonus, or increase advertising, or give it to customers as a discount.

Dealerships themselves won't advertise that they have dealer cash to spend, but with some online research, you can probably find the current dealer cash incentives. One disclaimer: just because it's on the internet doesn't mean it's true, so try to verify the facts before you use dealer cash as a negotiating tool.

If dealers have a lot of one model in stock, they might use dealer cash to lower the price on that model only. On the other hand, if they only have a few cars with dealer cash, they might not advertise the deal. If someone comes in to buy that particular model, however, salespeople know there's dealer cash available if they need room to maneuver to close the deal.

THE TRUTH ABOUT PROFIT MARGINS

Many people assume that dealerships make a huge profit on each new car sale. This may have been true in the past, but it's no longer the case. All aspects of manufacturing costs have increased (materials, production, marketing, employee incomes and pensions), and manufacturers have increased dealers' invoice prices as a result. However, the MSRP (manufacturer suggested retail price) has not increased at the same pace, so dealer profit margins have decreased.

In the 1960s and '70s, for example, dealer profit margins were around 22 percent. According to the National Auto Dealers Association, the average dealer markup in mid-2019 was 3 to 5 percent.[2] In other words, if a car has an MSRP of $30,000, 3 to 5 percent of that—or $900 to $1,500—is actual profit. To give you a couple real-world examples, figure 4.2 shows one of our invoices for a 2019 Kia Rio; figure 4.3 shows an invoice for a 2019 Kia Sorento. On the Rio, our profit was $464 (3 percent). On the Sorrento, it was $1,313 (4 percent).

apx 2% BELOW MSRP

MODEL/OPT 31422/010	DESCRIPTION KIA RIO LX	YEAR 2020	SERIAL NO. 3KPA24AD9LE266572	ENGINE NO. G4FMKE311216	MSRP	DEALER COST
EXT.CODE 4SS	W/P BOI OR SILKY SILVER	INT.CODE WK	INT.COLOR BLACK	KEY NO. KC2365	$15,750.00	$15,286.00

ADDITIONAL INSTALLED EQUIPMENT :

(In addition to or in place of standard features)

OPTIONS:

				SUBTOTAL	$15,750.00	$15,286.00
				OTHER CHARGES		
	ATTENTION:			INLAND FREIGHT & HANDLING	$925.00	$925.00

DEALER/FINANCING BANK - FOR REFERENCE
PURPOSES, PLEASE REFER TO ACH/DTC

MEMORANDUM INFORMATION ONLY THIS DOCUMENT DOES NOT TRANSFER TITLE	TOTAL	$16,675.00	$16,211.00

0016281108-303943-KRS0000-FPA0079

ORIGINAL

Figure 4.2. 2019 Kia Rio invoice

MODEL/OPT 74232/010	DESCRIPTION KIA SORENTO S FWD	YEAR 2019	SERIAL NO. 5XYPG4A54KG607821	ENGINE NO. G6DMJS830371	MSRP	DEALER COST
EXT.CODE DRB	EXT.COLOR DRAGON BROWN	INT.CODE WK	INT.COLOR BLACK	KEY NO. UM2893	$32,690.00	$31,415.00
ADDITIONAL INSTALLED EQUIPMENT :						
(In addition to or in place of standard features)						
OPTIONS:						
CM	Carpeted Floor Mats				$195.00	$157.00
			SUBTOTAL		$32,885.00	$31,572.00
			OTHER CHARGES			
ATTENTION:			INLAND FREIGHT & HANDLING		$1,045.00	$1,045.00
DEALER/FINANCING BANK - FOR REFERENCE PURPOSES, PLEASE REFER TO ACH/DTC						
MEMORANDUM INFORMATION ONLY THIS DOCUMENT DOES NOT TRANSFER TITLE			TOTAL		$33,930.00	$32,617.00

0016281200-708227-KRS0000-FPA0166

ORIGINAL

Figure 4.3. 2019 Kia Sorento invoice

What these invoices don't show is dealer holdback, which is the amount a manufacturer pays a dealer on every new vehicle sold. Holdback is usually 2 to 3 percent of the MSRP, and it is typically used to help offset fixed overhead expenses such as rent or utilities. On the Rio, for example, dealer holdback would be around $400, while it would be around $900 for the Sorento.

Some buyers try to use the dealer holdback to negotiate a lower price. If you try this, keep in mind the numbers shown here. Using holdback as a negotiating point might realistically save you hundreds of dollars, not thousands. Also keep in mind that some manufacturers have eliminated holdback altogether and that this is out of the dealership's control. You won't win any brownie points if you pester the salesperson about holdback after she has already told you there isn't any. (We'll talk about negotiating in more detail in chapter 6.)

If you're in the market for a new car, you have a lot to think about. It's an exciting time, but don't jump into this purchase without doing your research. If you're not in a place to buy a new car, used cars are a great option. The next chapter discusses the advantages of buying used as well as factors to consider before you shop.

CHAPTER 5

USED CARS

Frank was in the market for a used Ford F-150. He did his research and found a car online that met his SPACED (safety, performance, appearance, comfort, economy, dependability) criteria. It was a 2016 with 32,000 miles in the color he wanted with all the equipment he wanted at the price he wanted to pay. The only hang-up was that car sat on our lot in Ohio and he lived in North Carolina.

To Frank, that didn't matter. He bought a one-way ticket to Ohio, took an Uber to the dealership, bought the car, and drove thirteen hours back home. On the drive, he passed hundreds of dealerships, but none of them had the exact combination of features he was now enjoying.

Thirty years ago, Frank wouldn't have had the option of searching online to find the perfect car out of state. A guy in North Carolina would have no idea what cars were available five hundred miles away. The internet has completely changed the used car-buying game.

This chapter discusses how to use the World Wide Web to your advantage so you can get the best deal on the best used car for you and your family. It also provides factors to consider before you visit the dealership to buy a used car.

WHY BUY USED OVER NEW

The number one reason people buy used over new is price savings. Someone who couldn't afford a brand-new Cadillac might be able to buy a four-year-old model that's in excellent condition.

Another reason to buy used is that used cars don't depreciate like new cars. As soon as you drive a new car off the lot, it loses around 20 percent of its value. That number is even higher for luxury cars like Mercedes or Lexus. In addition to the initial hit, luxury cars lose an additional 10 percent during the first year of ownership. In total, a $30,000 car probably loses $9,000 in value in just one year. Depreciation in the first year is not nearly as high when you buy a used car. As a result, if you ever want to resell or trade in the used car, you will most likely sell it for closer to what you paid in the first place.

In general, cars are more dependable and reliable today,

so buying a used car doesn't automatically mean you're buying a money pit. Depending on how old the car is, it might even have some of the original manufacturer warranty left. Then you have the option of adding an Extended Service Contract so you're covered for a few more years/miles.

In many cases, car insurance is cheaper on used cars than on new cars. Depending on the state in which you live, you might also find that car registration is significantly cheaper on used cars.

HOW THE INTERNET HAS CHANGED THE GAME

One of the main ways the internet has changed the used-car buying game is in vehicle pricing. Up until the mid- to late 1990s, dealers could buy cars at auction or take trade-ins and mark them up to anything they deemed reasonable. Without widespread access to the internet, customers couldn't readily compare prices to find out whether they were getting a good deal. They could potentially search hard-copy sources such as *Consumer Reports*, the NADA (National Automobile Dealers Association) used car guide, or *Black Book*, but otherwise, used-car price information was limited. As a result, dealers had all the power.

Free used-car price guides like *AutoTrader* started appearing in print, and people could easily see what others were charging for comparable used cars. Now, websites such as Cars.com and Car Guru allow shoppers to type in the make and model, year, color, and miles they're looking for and find a list of cars for sale within those parameters. Comparing prices on used cars has never been easier.

As a result, the power has shifted to the consumer. People can narrow their search to a five- or fifty-mile radius of their hometown, or they can scan the entire United States. Think of Frank, who flew from North Carolina to Ohio because we had the Ford F-150 he wanted at a price he knew was reasonable. Dealerships can no longer mark up cars to ridiculous prices thinking someone will buy them. A local consumer can search the country in a matter of minutes and find out how ridiculous that dealer's price is.

Customers have told us, "Hey, I found this car. You have the same car, but there's another one 150 miles away at Dealership Y that's X dollars cheaper." As a dealer, we then have to decide whether we lower our price or tell the customer all the reasons she might not want to drive that far: you could get there and find out there's a five-inch poorly patched rip in the back seat, the passenger door is dented, the car smells like smoke, and so on. As a consumer, you have to decide if you're willing to pay more to get the car five miles away—a car you know is free of rips, dents, and smoke smell because you sat inside it and drove it around.

FACTORS TO CONSIDER

As with buying a new car, there are several factors to consider before you purchase a used car (in this chapter we're focusing on buying from a dealership, but many of these items apply to private-party purchases as well). Use the SPACED acronym from chapter 4 to think through what's most important: safety, performance, appearance, comfort, economy, or dependability. Even a used car is a major purchase, possibly your second biggest, so take time to figure out what's best for you.

In many ways, buying a new car is more straightforward—it's new, so the number of potential issues and complications is much lower. With used cars you need to consider age, miles, location, wear and tear, service records, and much more. If you're willing to do your research, however, you can end up with a safe, reliable car for far less money than you would pay for something new.

INSPECTIONS

When buying a used car, one of the biggest concerns is maintenance. Cars are made up of moving parts that break down over time; that's just a fact. Before you invest in a used vehicle, find out as much as you can about its service history.

Start by asking to see the report the dealer has pulled from CARFAX or AutoCheck. This report should have most of the following information, but just in case, here are some specific questions to ask:

- How many previous owners has the car had?
- Has it been in an accident?
- Has it been properly serviced and/or regularly maintained? Is there documented proof that each service was performed?
- Was it a fleet car or rental?
- What is the original in-service date of the vehicle? (The in-service date is the date the manufacturer recognizes as the warranty start date. Knowing the in-service date will let you know if the car still has any of the original manufacturer's warranty remaining.)
- Does the vehicle have a clean title? (You want a car with a clean title, not a salvage title. A car with a salvage title has been previously deemed a total loss because of flood, accident, or other damage.)

Unless you're buying an as-is vehicle (more on as-is cars later in the chapter), the dealership should provide the multipoint inspection sheet performed on the car. If they don't, ask for it. After reading this report, take the vehicle to your mechanic to get a second opinion. (Note: You won't be able to do this if you buy out of town, though you could take it to a local mechanic.)

ACCIDENT REPORTS

As part of your initial inspection, check the car through websites such as CARFAX and AutoCheck to find out if it's been in accidents. Keep in mind, however, that these reports are not 100 percent accurate. We sold a car that we had run through AutoCheck, which showed no accidents. Afterward, something about the car caused the owner to think it had been in an accident. She called us, and we ran the car through CARFAX. Sure enough, the report showed it had been in not one, but three accidents.

One possible reason for differences between reports is that there are different levels of accidents, and the level is typically determined by what's reported under your insurance. Let's say your car is parked in your driveway and the wind blows over your portable basketball hoop and it dents your hood. You report it to the insurance company, who pays the local body shop to fix it. CARFAX might list that incident as an accident because insurance work was done on the vehicle, even though a basketball hoop falling on your hood isn't a car-to-car accident. The same might apply if you back into a cement pillar in a parking garage, and the insurance pays to have the back bumper replaced. CARFAX might count that as an accident, whereas AutoCheck might not.

Even with the potential inconsistencies, it's better to be aware of what might have happened to any car you're considering.

LOCAL VERSUS OUT OF TOWN

When you buy a car from out of state or out of town, you're probably on your own if the car has mechanical issues. You're not going to get much help from a dealership that's a hundred miles away.

On the flip side, if you buy a used vehicle from a local dealer and something happened within the first week, you might get some help. Perhaps they missed something during inspection, or it was simply a moving part that reached the end of its life. The dealer will most likely want to do what they can to keep you happy as a long-term customer.

THE LOWEST PRICE ISN'T ALWAYS THE BEST DEAL

Some dealers buy salvage title cars—vehicles that have been deemed a total loss by insurance companies—and then send them to an auto body shop to get fixed up. Salvage cars are definitely not worth the same as used cars that simply have a lot of miles.

With salvage cars, the biggest question is, where did that car come from? Was it in a flood? If so, it might have electrical issues and it might rust sooner than a comparable car. During seasons with hurricanes and flooding in states such as Florida, insurance companies can't keep up with the overwhelming number of wrecked cars. Before the insurance companies can officially record cars as a total loss, some dealers buy these vehicles dirt cheap, put in new carpet, and turn around and sell them without ever disclosing they were in a flood.

Dealers can also buy rental cars from companies such as Avis, Hertz, and Enterprise, and then sell them as used cars. Those cars might be cheaper, but they will typically have very high miles. They may have been driven harder as well. A single-owner used car with 20,000 miles put on over two years is likely in better shape than a rental with 20,000 put on in one year.

DIGITAL SHOWROOM

The internet is now a digital showroom for used cars. You can look at thousands of cars with the click of a mouse. Knowing this, most dealers take multiple photos of any car they're selling, from multiple angles, trying to show every aspect of the car so the customer can see the quality of the product. Dealerships know they're competing with thousands of other sellers in this new digital world.

If a dealer has one or two pictures of a car, however, beware. Not showing every angle of the car probably means there's something to hide. Perhaps the unseen door has a huge dent or the right bumper is missing some paint.

WARRANTIES AND EXTENDED SERVICE CONTRACTS

New cars come with manufacturer warranties that usually last three to five years (36,000 to 60,000 miles). In many cases, these warranties are transferable. That means if you buy a three- to five-year-old car, it might still have some of the original warranty remaining. If the dealer doesn't offer this information, be sure to ask.

Whether or not the used car is still under warranty, you have the option of buying an Extended Service Contract (ESC). If the car is under warranty, the ESC will extend your coverage. If not, the ESC acts like a warranty for your used car.

As with warranties, you have several options when it comes to ESCs. You can get a contract that covers the power train only (transmission, engine, etc.), or you can buy the basic bumper-to-bumper version. The available terms and miles depend on the current age and miles on the car, as well as how long you plan to drive the vehicle. Whichever ESC you choose, the cost can be wrapped into the car payment if you are financing the purchase.

No matter how much you pay for your car or how old it is, it's still an investment. It makes sense to protect it. Chapter 8 provides more details on ESCs and other ways to protect your investment.

AS-IS CARS

As-is cars come with what old-timers call the "Oklahoma guarantee": if it breaks in half, you own both halves. They are generally older, high-mileage cars that might have been slated for auction. Because of their age and miles, these vehicles don't have available warranties or ESCs and are sold as is, which is exactly what it sounds like.

Some dealers clearly mark as-is cars and others don't. If you're considering an older, high-mileage car, ask the salesperson if it comes with any warranty. If not, that probably means it's being sold as-is, but you should ask just to make sure.

If you buy an as-is car, remember that when it breaks down,

you can't go back and complain to the dealer or demand that they fix whatever broke. You may have signed several forms indicating that you understand the car is being sold as is, period. Some forms might even ask you to agree not to blast the dealer on social media if the car breaks down. In every way possible, the forms you sign basically say, "We don't want to sell you this car. Please don't buy it."

Dealers might put as-is cars through a safety inspection, but it won't be the detailed fifty-one-point service inspection newer used cars receive. Dealers will make sure the car stops when the brakes are applied, that there's at least some tire tread left, and the car starts when you turn the key. They will also check the headlights and taillights, but that's about it. You could take the car to your mechanic for an inspection to know what you are getting into, but it could be a waste of money because most dealers wouldn't fix anything that was found. As is means as is.

Nonetheless, as-is cars serve a purpose. Maybe you have a nice Dodge truck, but it only gets sixteen miles to the gallon. For $2,000 to $3,000, you could buy a fuel-efficient go-to-work car. The key is to remember what you're getting: an as-is vehicle that's likely not attractive and not destined for a long life.

CERTIFIED PRE-OWNED

While as-is cars might be considered a step down from most used cars, Certified Pre-Owned (CPO) cars might be considered a step up. Many manufacturers sell CPO cars. Honda and Lexus, for example, have excellent CPO programs.

To be certified, used cars go through a rigorous multipoint inspection and safety check. Hyundai's CPO inspection checklist, for instance, has over two hundred items covering the exterior, interior, maintenance, tires, and more. Certified used cars also have to meet certain qualifications in terms of age and miles. For example, CPO cars can't be more than five years old or have more than 60,000 miles.

As you can imagine, CPO cars are more expensive, partly because it costs the dealer money to certify the car through the manufacturer. At the same time, dealerships often have attractive finance options on CPOs, similar to what you might find with a new car. In addition, CPOs sometimes come with a better warranty than noncertified used cars. As with other used cars, you have the option of extending the warranty with an ESC.

Some people like buying CPO cars because they're spending less than they would on a new car, but they're still getting the assurance that the car is in good condition. It's a nice middle option between a brand-new car that's going to depreciate as soon as you drive it off the lot and a used car with an unknown service history.

NO CRYSTAL BALL

Buying a used car is like going to the doctor. You might get a physical and hear that you are 100 percent healthy, and then two weeks later you catch a cold. Most people don't blame the doctor for not telling them they were going to get sick in a couple of weeks. They understand that when the doctor evaluated them, they were healthy. The doc doesn't have a crystal ball to predict that someone will fall sick soon after.

Consider a similar situation involving a used car. You go into the dealership and buy a used car. According to the multipoint inspection report and your personal mechanic, the car checks out. No major issues can be found. Two weeks later, however, the check engine light comes on. What is your natural reaction?

In this situation, people are more likely to blame the dealership, even though the scenario is not much different than visiting a doctor and then falling ill. Dealerships don't have a crystal ball. They don't know when a car is suddenly going to develop a problem. As mentioned, cars have a lot of moving parts and they break down. It happens every day, even if the car was "healthy" according to its multipoint inspection.

Remember, you're buying a *used* car. Things happen. There's no way to predict if something is going to break one week, three weeks, or two months after you buy the vehicle.

Also, most dealers will not try to cheat you or sell you a used car with problems. Dealers want to build a long-term relationship with you in the hopes that you will bring that car to the service department when it does have issues. They're also hoping you will keep them in mind for future car purchases, whether used or new.

In the next chapter, we'll discuss how to enter this dealer-customer relationship in a positive way.

CHAPTER 6

NEGOTIATING

Bridget walks into the dealership looking for help. She's feeling a little nervous because she's never bought a car before, so her friend Tami has come along for moral support.

Salesman Rick sees Bridget and Tami wandering around and walks up to greet them. "Hi, I'm Rick," he says with a smile and sticks out his hand. "Can I help you?"

"Hi, I'm Bridget," she says as she shakes Rick's hand. "This is Tami," she says, pointing to her friend. "I'm here because I heard your radio ad for a Kia Rio for a hundred and ninety-nine dollars."

"Great!" says Rick. "Now, that price is for a three-year lease on a Rio. Are you looking to lease?"

"Oh," she says and then pauses. "I don't know. I've never leased a car. I think I'd rather buy. Plus, I'm kinda on a budget and a hundred and ninety-nine dollars was perfect."

"No problem. We can still look at the Rio and see if we can get a low enough payment. Let's go take a look at one."

After taking a test drive, they go inside to talk numbers.

"How does three hundred twenty-five dollars a month sound?" Rick asks.

"Oh, geez. You know, I had a budget of two hundred dollars a month. I don't know if I can afford that. Is there anything we can do to bring it down?"

"Well, you could put more money down. Is that possible?"

"Hmm. I could come up with a thousand dollars."

"OK," Rick says as he taps on his calculator. "What do you think about a longer-term loan? If you do seventy-two months instead of sixty, we can get the payment down to two hundred and forty-five dollars."

After the paperwork is signed, Rick says, "Let's get a photo in front of your new car!" As Tami takes the picture, she says, "You two make a cute couple. You should go out." Rick and Bridget look at each other and kind of laugh. Then Rick says, "What are you doing next Saturday?" True story: they married a year later.

Many people hate the whole car-buying and negotiating process because they think they're going to get ripped off. As a result, they come in with their guard up, ready to fight— instead of looking for someone to guide them through the process. In doing so, they set the salesperson on edge and get the whole relationship off to bad start.

Bridget heard the radio ad and came in thinking the $199 deal applied to purchases. She was disappointed when she found out that wasn't the case, but she didn't become angry and argumentative. She didn't assume she was being duped by a bait-and-switch (she actually misunderstood the ad). Bridget came in with the attitude of "I'm here to buy a car. Guide me through the process." Even though she didn't get what she initially hoped for, she stayed respectful, listened to the options Rick offered, and ultimately left happy with her purchase.

In this chapter, we'll discuss ways to approach negotiating that will give you a more positive car-buying experience and ultimately achieve better results. I can't guarantee you'll get a spouse out of the deal, but I can promise you'll save time and be more at ease if you follow these negotiating guidelines. Who knows? You might actually have fun!

BE PREPARED

The number one tip for headache-free negotiating is to come prepared. Whether you're looking at new or used cars, research your options ahead of time so you know what you want. Check your credit score and play around with an online loan calculator. Know what your financial situation looks like so you know what you can pay every month and how much you can put down up front. Know the approximate wholesale value of your trade-in, if you have one. If you haven't done these things ahead of time, you're probably not prepared to negotiate or buy a car.

We often hear that customers hate how much time it takes to buy a car, yet we regularly sell cars to people in an hour or less. The key is that these people are prepared. They call us and say something like, "I saw this ad. I want this car. And I'm coming in tomorrow at three o'clock." When they arrive, they meet the salesperson, test-drive the car, meet with finance, and they're driving off the lot an hour after they arrive.

The people who spend all day at the dealership are those who haven't done their research, so they don't know what they want. They test-drive three or four cars, and after they decide which one they want, they discover that they have negative equity on their trade-in and their credit score is 150 points lower than they thought, so finance has to work doubly hard and still can't get them approved. Then the customers get upset because they've spent all day at the dealership and have no car to show for it.

If these customers would have come prepared—knowing they have negative equity and bad credit and that they couldn't get a $30,000 SUV for $200 a month—they could have avoided this miserable, back-and-forth, all-day process.

TAYLOR TIP

Be prepared to leave. Let's say you've done your homework. You know the car you want, you know the approximate value of your trade-in, and you know you can budget a maximum of $400 a month for a car payment.

However, after negotiating with finance and asking about potential rebates and special interest rates, the dealer still can't get you to less than $550 a month. It's OK to leave the dealership. If the monthly payment is outside your financial comfort zone, it's OK to say, "Thank you for your time, but I can't do that."

BE REALISTIC

As a caveat to being prepared and knowing your budget, you have to be realistic. Some customers come in, look at a $30,000 vehicle, and want to spend $300 a month on a car payment. As discussed earlier, simple math tells you the minimum payment would be $500 a month, and that's before interest and taxes. Having realistic expectations will make for smoother negotiations.

Also be realistic regarding how much a dealer can lower the price from a profit standpoint. Remember what we said in chapter 4 about the decreasing profit margins. Dealers truly have only so much wiggle room. They are businesses, and businesses have to make a profit to stay in business. If a salesperson says she can't go lower than a certain price, it's probably true.

As part of your preparation, check online to see if you can find out manufacturer invoice versus MSRP on the model you're considering. This will give you a realistic picture of the dealer's markup or profit margin. If you know the dealer is making $900 on a certain car, you're probably not going to successfully negotiate a $2,000 discount.

Understanding the dealership's position, you might approach negotiation something like this: "I understand you guys are here to make money. I just don't want you to club me over the head like a baby seal. I'm willing to pay $___ over invoice."

Keep in mind you're paying the state a certain percentage in sales tax—probably at least 6 percent. Is it reasonable for the dealer to make 2.5 to 3 percent profit?

Also remember that if a salesperson spent four hours with you, and the finance manager spent another four hours talking to the bank and structuring a deal, and they still can't get you to the monthly payment you want, it's not because they don't want to. They are highly invested at that point. They want to work out a deal that allows you to buy the car because that's how they make money. No one wants to work for free. If dealers don't sell cars, they don't make money. Period.

REBATES, DEALER CASH, AND INCENTIVIZED INTEREST RATES

On any given car, there might be a manufacturer rebate and an incentivized (usually very low) interest rate. In most cases, you get one: the $3,000 rebate *or* 0 percent financing. Keep this in mind when you're negotiating.

To figure out which is the better deal, find an online payment calculator. Put in the selling price without the rebate at the incentivized rate (for example, 0 percent or 1.9 percent) for the available term. Then discount the selling price by the amount of the rebate and figure the payments given an interest rate you'd likely qualify for given your credit (this assumes you've already discovered your credit score). Once you're in the dealership, ask the salesperson to run the numbers and compare them with what you found online. You could say something like, "I'd like to see my payments with the incentivized interest rate and with the rebate and the interest rate I qualify for."

Incentivized interest rates often have a shorter term, for example, twenty-four or thirty-six months instead of the usual sixty or seventy-two months. Because shorter terms usually have higher monthly payments, even with a lower interest rate, you may decide to go with the rebate so you can get the longer term and lower monthly payments.

Also keep in mind that the rebates are from the manufacturer. Don't haggle with the salesperson over a rebate. They don't control the amount.

If you've done your research and discovered that the dealer should have a rebate or dealer cash on the model you're looking at, bring it up when you visit. Keep in mind, however, that you can't trust everything you read online. While writing this book, I looked for dealer cash on Kia models, just to see what was out there on the Web. I found one website that said there was $5,100 dealer cash on the Kia Optima. I emailed my sales manager, who replied, "That's crazy! I wish we had that kind of money." Kia was not offering dealer cash on the Optima that month, let alone $5,100 worth.

Even if manufacturer rebate discounts are available, they typically don't amount to thousands of dollars anymore. Be realistic about how much markdown you expect. If you think you can get a $5,000 discount on a $20,000 Kia Rio, you'll likely be disappointed.

BE NICE

The next tip is pretty simple: be nice. Obey the Golden Rule and treat salespeople the way you want to be treated. You're going to get a lot further with a salesperson when you're working *with* them and not against them.

Salespeople in general often get a bad rap because people still view them as being like Merle from the opening story: sleazy, manipulative, and deaf to what the customer really wants. As a result, customers come into a dealership with a defensive attitude, thinking salespeople are out to take advantage of them. Some customers are downright rude and disrespectful.

One of my sales managers said, "As a well-armed buyer, you want all the numbers from the dealer: interest rate, term, cost, trade value, rebates, et cetera. You'll only get them if you're nice to the sales rep." Knowing those numbers will help you in a negotiation, but salespeople may not be motivated to share them with you if you're disrespectful.

BE RESPECTFUL OF TIME

Be respectful of the salesperson's time. If you call ahead and set up an appointment with a salesman, be there—or at least call to say you can't make it.

One customer emailed our dealership to say he was looking at a certain car and wanted to come in with his wife to look at it at 6:00 p.m. on a Monday night. The salesperson told him the car would be pulled up and ready. At 7:30, they still hadn't arrived, so the salesperson called.

"Oh, we can't make it tonight," was his reply.

Would you do that with your doctor, dentist, attorney, or

any other professional with whom you had an appointment? Probably not. You would at least call to say you're going to be late or that you have to cancel. Yet it happens every day to car salespeople. They block off time knowing a customer is coming in, only to have the person not show. That's a real blow if they're earning income based on commission; they could have been helping someone else buy a car instead of waiting. Salespeople try to be respectful of your time; do the same for them.

UNDERSTAND THAT CASH IS NOT KING

Your grandfather may have given you this tip: "When you go in, tell them you've got five thousand dollars cash to buy a car." Forty or fifty years ago, having cash may have gotten you a better deal or a bigger discount, but not anymore. In fact, dealerships often encourage people not to pay cash. It doesn't make sense to pay cash on something that's a depreciating asset. Instead, put $2,000 down, get a loan, and put the other $3,000 in an investment account to earn money over the next six years.

Offering to write a check for $10,000 cash is not going to help in negotiating a better price; neither is offering $20,000 cash for a $25,000 car. Cash doesn't help the dealer. In fact, the dealership actually benefits more if someone finances the car. Offering cash is not a wise negotiating point, no matter what your grandfather may have told you.

WAIT UNTIL THE END OF THE MONTH

While offering cash is a negotiating myth, waiting until the end of the month is not. You actually might get a better deal if you go into the dealership on the last day of the month.

Manufacturers sometimes offer new car volume incentives in which dealers receive cash if the goal number of sales is reached. This bonus is often a per-car amount that is retroactive to unit one, meaning the dealer would receive the money on every car sold back to the beginning of the month.

If a dealer needs to sell three cars on the last day of the month to meet that goal, they might take a skinnier deal on those three cars, knowing they will be receiving a lot more in return because they met the incentive.

MENTION YOUR TRADE-IN UP FRONT

Trade-ins are complex, and they often become a major sticking point in negotiations. Most people think their trade-in is worth more than it is—or at least more than the dealer wants to figure in terms of the current deal.

Because trade-ins can be such a big variable in negotiations, we've dedicated the next chapter to this topic. At this point, the most important thing to remember is to be up front about your trade-in. You won't win any friends if the salesperson has spent time showing you cars and structuring a deal, only to have you surprise him with the fact that you have a trade-in.

(handwritten note: SOUNDS LIKE GOOD ADVICE)

THROW OUT THE FIRST NUMBER

This may seem counterintuitive, but it's true: whoever throws out the first number wins the negotiation. If a customer comes in and says she wants to spend $300 a month on a payment, the salesperson's job and the entire negotiation process revolves around that number. The same happens if the customer says he wants a certain amount for his trade-in or a certain final price on the car.

Many customers are reluctant to throw out a number. They wait for the salesperson to tell them what the payments will be, and then it becomes a standoff. Throwing out the first number actually helps the negotiation process and gives you more power. Now the salesperson is doing everything possible to reach your magic number.

My advice: throw out your number early in the negotiation process. If you want to save time and avoid stress, don't wait until the end. If the salesperson had known your number up front, he could have taken a different route. Using simple math, he could have told you three hours ago that you will not be able to get into X car with Y monthly payment (remember the triangle!).

SLOW DOWN

Some customers come in hot. They want (demand) to know the selling price, interest rate, term, money down, and amount for their trade-in before they've taken two steps onto the lot.

My recommendation is to slow down. Let the salesperson help you make sure you want to own the car you're asking about, before you both go through all the trouble of making the deal work financially. You might drive the car and hate it or realize you really want a crossover and not a truck.

COMPARE APPLES TO APPLES

Part of negotiating is bringing comparable prices from one dealership into your discussions with another. Before you do that, however, make sure you're comparing like products.

Some dealers may advertise a certain price and say the car includes certain things, when in actuality it's a stripped-down model that includes none of the things you want. Find this out *before* you start hardballing another dealer. Make absolutely sure you're talking apples to apples. If you find out that other dealership was being shady or didn't give full info, you may come back with egg on your face.

This is another reason to be respectful in all negotiations. If you buy a certain car from a dealership outside your town, chances are you're going to take it to the local dealer for service. If you were a jerk during negotiations, the local dealer might not be as eager to help you. That's just a fact of life.

TAYLOR TIP

When you come into the dealership, leave your kids at home or find someone to watch them. Your kids probably don't want to be there, and you're going to get frustrated if you're trying to negotiate while they are whining. You're talking about a major financial decision. Make sure you can give 100 percent focus to the task at hand, instead of dividing your attention between the salesperson and your kids running around the showroom causing trouble.

Negotiating is part of the car-buying process, and it doesn't haven't to be a miserable, time-consuming experience. If you do your homework and remember the Golden Rule, you're likely to spend less time at the dealership and come away with friends you can count on for the life of your car.

If you have a trade-in to include as part of your financing deal, remember to mention it early in the process. The next chapter provides tips for making sure you have realistic expectations regarding your trade-in's value and for considering whether you might sell it on your own instead.

CHAPTER 7

TRADE-INS

Despite my warning regarding the hassles involved in selling a used car, my buddy Jason decided to give it a shot. He bought all the supplies needed to clean and detail his Honda Accord, and he spent all Saturday washing, waxing, vacuuming, and polishing. Then he listed his car for $6,000 on Craigslist, Autotrader, and even eBay.

Within a couple days, the calls started rolling in. When they did, however, they started sucking up his time at work. People called with questions about the current odometer reading, the accident history, if anyone had ever smoked in the car—all the normal questions someone would ask before they buy a used car.

Jason didn't want people coming to his house to see the car, so he arranged to meet one potential buyer at a Denny's restaurant parking lot. The guy seemed really interested, so when he wanted to meet at ten o'clock at night, Jason agreed. Shortly before ten, however, the buyer called and said he couldn't get the cash together and asked to meet Jason at midnight.

"All right," Jason said. "I'll meet you at midnight. But are you sure you're coming?"

"Yeah, yeah. We're coming," the guy replied.

Just before midnight, however, Jason received another call. "Hey, we're running late. We'll be there by two o'clock."

At this point, Jason began to worry that he was getting set up. He made up this whole story in his head, that these guys were going to come down to the Denny's, give him the cash, and then someone was going to pop out of another car, shoot him, and leave him to bleed out in the middle of the parking lot.

"Listen," Jason said to the buyer after this scenario ran through his head. "You said ten, then midnight, and now two. I don't want to be in the middle of a Denny's parking lot getting six thousand dollars cash at two in the morning. I'm not doing this."

The next day, Jason called me and said, "You're never going

to believe this." Then he paused and said, "Well, yeah, you will."

Before he started the whole process of cleaning and listing his car, Jason had asked my advice, and I told him it wasn't worth it. "Sure, you might get a little more money, but you have to clean it. You have to take pictures. You have to meet the person and make sure they have the cash. It's not worth it. You're better off trading it in at the dealership."

In the end, Jason sold his Accord to someone else, in the middle of the day, for less than $6,000. And he agreed, it wasn't worth it.

If it's such a hassle, why do people bother selling their used car on their own? Because 99.9 percent of the time, they can make more money than if they traded it in at the dealership. That's a fact even dealerships don't try to hide.

However, as Jason found out, so many other factors go into selling on your own. Some of you may decide the extra money is worth the effort; others may not. This chapter will help you weigh the two options so you can decide if you want to sell on your own or trade in at the dealership.

SELLING ON YOUR OWN

I'll say it again: you will most likely get more money for your car if you sell it on your own. That's a given. You simply have to decide if the time and potential stress are worth the extra cash.

TIME

In terms of time commitment, selling on your own involves a lot of little things. To put your car in the best light and get top dollar, you'll want to wash, vacuum, and possibly wax it. If the upholstery is stained, you'll want to spot clean it. Don't forget to wipe down the interior and clean out stray gum wrappers and other trash.

Even if you advertise your car on free websites only, it's still going to cost you time in taking photos, posting them, and writing an ad. You will also spend time answering phone calls and showing the car.

Jason had people meeting him at work to see the car, so he had to stop and go meet the potential buyer in the parking lot. He also had to deal with people who set up appointments and then didn't show up, not to mention the time he spent test-driving with potential customers.

STRESS

When you finally have a potential buyer, the person will probably want to negotiate a lower price. You might want $6,000 but chances are, a buyer won't want to pay that. How low are you willing to go? Does haggling over price make you anxious?

Potential buyers will want to test-drive the car, but that means they're driving on your insurance. You don't know this guy from Adam. What do you do? Do you get a copy of his driver's license? Do you check to make sure he has insurance?

How are you going to handle the service side? If someone notices the left rear taillight is out, they may want to know if you're going to fix it or reduce the price. They will ask if there's anything wrong with the car. If you say the car is great and then something happens two days after you sell it, the customer is likely going to call and ask for their money back or ask you to do something to fix the problem.

Then you have to worry about getting paid. Are you comfortable handling a large amount of cash? Do you trust someone to write you a check? Do you want to worry about going to the bank and handling a certified check? Certified checks are certainly safer than personal checks, but it might also take longer to actually receive the funds because of the certification process.

You can use online services such as PayPal and Venmo, but some charge fees and others have limits on how much can be transferred.

TRADING IN AT THE DEALERSHIP

If you're looking for a hassle-free or at least less headache-prone experience, selling on your own is probably not the way to go. Trading it in at the dealership will definitely be less time-consuming and likely less stressful. Still, there are some things to keep in mind.

BE REALISTIC ABOUT THE CONDITION

This is probably the most important point to remember with your trade-in. There are websites to help you evaluate what your car is worth, but to get a realistic number, you have to input realistic information.

Most people think their car is in excellent condition. If you mark excellent, the estimate you'll get online will likely be higher than what a dealer will offer when they see your car in person, which might cause unnecessary stress.

The Kelley Blue Book website, for example, has four categories for rating your used car's condition: fair, good, very good, and excellent. As a guideline, they give a percentage of how many cars they value fall into each of these categories:

- Fair: 19 percent
- Good: 55 percent
- Very good: 23 percent
- Excellent: 3 percent

That should give you an idea of how many used cars are actually in excellent condition, despite what their owners think.

Another factor in determining the condition and therefore value of your car is the miles. The question on these websites is usually worded something like "Does your car have an average number of miles for a car its age?" The average per year is around 12,000 miles, so a three-year-old car would have around 36,000 miles. If your car has a lot more than that, it will be worth less than a car with the average or less. The number of miles affects condition; high miles can lower the condition to average or below average. Mileage matters much more than dents and scratches in determining the condition of your car.

Tread and condition of the tires also affects overall condition of the car. Dealers want to know if they're going to have to replace the tires; that adds to their cost in preparing to resell the car.

Average wear and tear are expected on a used car. Minor dents, dings, and scratches are OK, but major body damage—collision-type damage—will greatly affect the value of the car. Likewise, minor stains on the upholstery are fine because dealers can easily clean those, but rips and major stains will affect the value.

If the dashboard is lit up like a Christmas tree—check engine light, air pressure light, and so on—that will definitely affect the value of your car.

BE UP FRONT ABOUT HAVING A TRADE-IN

If you've ever read one of those articles about "10 Ways to Save Money the Next Time You Buy a Car," number 7 or 8 is usually something like "Don't tell the dealer you have a trade-in until the very end." As mentioned in chapter 6, this is bad advice. You should mention having a trade-in early in your discussion.

Withholding information about a trade-in makes people feel like they're getting one up on the dealer. If you're trying to develop a relationship with a salesperson, however, this is a lousy tactic. It might get you more money, but it will more likely anger the salesperson and finance person who have spent hours helping you find a car and structure a deal that gives you the rate you want. This is not the way to create a headache-free buying experience.

If you come in and tell the salesperson up front that you

have a trade-in, the appraisal process can start immediately. If you still owe money on the trade-in, the finance manager can call the bank to get the payoff amount. With the payoff amount and the value for your trade-in, the finance manager can figure out if you have negative equity. When the facts and figures are known up front, these can be taken into account as your deal is being structured.

On the other hand, if the finance person has structured the deal, called the bank, and laid out your monthly payments and then finds out you have $6,000 in negative equity, she has to start all over.

This is when people often become upset because now their time at the dealership is extended—time that could have been avoided if they were up front about the trade-in.

Mentioning the trade-in at the last minute could also cost you money. You're not winning friends by playing games with the salesperson. It's quite likely that you'll get less for your trade-in if you bring it to the table after they've spent a good chunk of time structuring a deal. Whereas you may have received $5,000 originally, suddenly that car could be worth thousands less.

WHAT HAPPENS ON THE DEALER'S SIDE

Every time dealers accept a trade-in, they take a risk.

They need to appraise the vehicle accurately so they have enough profit markup wiggle room to service the car, detail it, advertise it, and pay a salesperson to sell it—while still turning a profit (dealerships are businesses, after all). All of these things cost money, on top of the money given to the person trading in the car. Plus, many trade-ins are sent straight to auction because they have so many problems.

If your trade-in has an undesirable or unpopular color combination, it may not sell quickly. In the world of dealerships, that's bad. Dealers want to constantly move inventory. They keep track of cars that are over thirty, sixty, or ninety days old, and they typically discount cars the older they get. Any car sitting on the lot is tying up dealership cash that could be buying new inventory or in the bank earning interest.

TAYLOR TIP

If you trade in at the dealership, don't forget the extra key or key fob. It used to be that dealers simply had to cut a second key, but now they have to buy a fob, which is usually a few hundred dollars. Then a technician has to program it. If the customer has both keys, we might give them an extra $300 for their car because we avoid the hassle of getting secondary fobs made.

GETTING YOU THE BEST DEAL

Back in the day, dealers used the NADA used car guide or the *Black Book* to help them determine a fair trade-in price. The *Black Book* was published by region—West Coast, Midwest, Southeast, Northeast—and prices were based on auction data. The books changed every month or so, and dealers made their best guess at a vehicle's value based on the most recent average auction data.

Today, dealers use real-time data-driven software that gives them a much more precise number based on that car's specific data. They can type in a vehicle's VIN (vehicle identification number), mileage, equipment, and so on. They can see how many of that specific vehicle have sold in their market and in the country. They can see average price and what's a hot car right now. For example, if everyone is suddenly in the market for a fuel-efficient four-door sedan, prices will go through the roof and supply will become scarce. Dealers know they can put more money in that car because they will be able to sell it faster and for more money.

This software and the information it generates benefit the customer because dealers can put a more scientific number to the appraisal and give the customer more money for their trade-in as a result.

If you decide to take a chance like Jason did and sell your car on your own, go for it! If you decide to trade it in at the dealer, be sure to do your homework ahead of time so you aren't disappointed at the appraisal. Whether you buy new or used after selling your old car, you'll want to protect that new investment. Chapter 8 discusses the top ways to do so.

PROTECTING YOUR INVESTMENT

Jim purchased his 2012 GMC Terrain from Taylor Automotive in 2016. For an additional forty-one dollars a month, he purchased a Power Train Extended Service Contract.

Two years later, Jim brought his vehicle in to the service department because it was idling rough. After the service adviser looked it over, he determined Jim's car needed a whole new engine to the tune of $4,252. Because Jim had purchased the power train service contract, his share of the expense was simply his fifty-dollar deductible. He was very happy he took his finance manager's suggestion!

A Power Train Extended Service Contract is one of many options for protecting your vehicle investment. When they're offered a service contract like this, many people say no out of habit either because they've heard these products are a scam or they think they're too expensive. In this chapter, you'll get a brief overview of the main products dealerships provide, and you'll hear how they helped several real-life customers save hundreds or thousands of dollars.

THE AUTOMATIC NO

As I've said, a car—whether new or used—is one of the most expensive purchases you'll make. Why wouldn't you want to protect it? People buy protection plans for their $500 or $800 cell phone, but they are hesitant to buy products to cover their $20,000 vehicle, which has far more moving parts and has much more costly repairs.

One reason people don't get these protections is they think they can't afford them. The truth is, you can't afford not to have them. If your car breaks down and you can't afford to fix it, you might be tempted to stop making payments. If you stop making payments, the car could be repossessed, which will affect your credit. If you don't have a car to drive to work, you could get fired. This is an extreme example, but car troubles without proper protection can spell financial ruin. For a few extra dollars per day on your loan, this situation could be prevented with an Extended Service Contract.

The second reason people automatically say no is that have been taught these products are unnecessary. The reflex reaction is "No, I don't need a service contract," whether it's on a washing machine, vacuum cleaner, or car.

People also view these products as money-making schemes for the dealership. They've probably read the article with "10 Tips on How to Save Money When Buying a Car," with one tip being "Don't buy any of the products that the dealer's going to sell you. You don't need them or they're no good. They're not worth the paper they're printed on."

Do dealerships make money when they sell these products? Yes, but not as much as you might think. If a dealership sells an Extended Service Contract for $3,500, they might make $700.

I could provide hundreds of testimonials from our dealerships alone, each of which says something like "I bought an Extended Service Contract and I used it for a $4,000 repair and only paid the $50 deductible" or "I bought a Tire and Wheel Protection plan and used it and got a free tire."

Since you're reading this book, why not take the time to learn about some of these products? Then when you go into the dealership, you'll know what to expect when the salesperson asks if you want to learn more. One day you might be glad that you didn't automatically say no.

PRODUCTS AVAILABLE

The three most common products people purchase to protect their investment are the Extended Service Contract (ESC), GAP (Guaranteed Asset Protection) coverage, and Tire and Wheel Protection. We'll discuss each of these, and then summarize two others you might hear about while at the dealership. One interesting note is that most lenders typically allow the addition of these products without preapproval because they add protection for your mutual investment.

EXTENDED SERVICE CONTRACT

Cory purchased his 2008 GMC Acadia from Taylor Automotive in 2017, and with it he purchased an Extended Service Contract that cost him forty-three dollars a month. Eighteen months later, he started experiencing issues that made his vehicle unreliable. It wouldn't start at times and left him stranded once. Because he had the service contract, $4,135 of the $4,185 invoice was covered. Cory simply had to pay his fifty-dollar deductible.

* * *

Natasha purchased her new 2018 Kia Optima from Taylor Automotive, and within ten months, she lost her key fob for keyless entry. She had purchased the maximum Extended Service Contract, which covered the cost of buying and programming her new fob. Natasha was ecstatic, not realizing that the contract was so comprehensive and would take care of that type of loss too.

* * *

Tony purchased a used 2016 Hyundai Tucson from Taylor Automotive after seeing it listed on the internet. Because the Tucson was used, Tony decided to buy the Extended Service Contract. Down the road, he noticed the engine sounded strange and wasn't running as smoothly as it had been. When all was said and done, the engine repairs totaled $4,200 and they were all covered by his contract. Since he paid $1,500 for the contract originally, Tony was very happy with the return.

As stated in chapter 5, an Extended Service Contract (ESC) is a maintenance agreement that prolongs the standard warranty that comes with the car you buy. You can purchase an ESC for a new or used car. In both cases, it provides protection against costly repairs, such as those highlighted in the preceding Happy Customer stories.

The type of ESC that's best for you depends on your driving habits and how long you plan to own the car. Someone who plans to drive a car until the wheels fall off will want a different plan than someone who is going to keep the car for only a couple years.

The cost of an ESC depends on its length in months and miles, as well as what is covered. In general, ESCs run about twenty-five to fifty dollars a month. Some plans cover the power train only, and some include roadside assistance and replacement of key fobs (as Natasha found out).

Here's how an ESC works: You might have a five-year, 60,000-mile warranty that covers a part such as the touch screen that controls your radio, climate, and other electronics. If that part breaks after the warranty has expired, you would have to pay to have it fixed. A touch screen repair, or replacement, might cost $2,500. If you have an ESC, however, the repair would be covered. Instead of paying $2,500, you would simply pay the deductible, which could be zero dollars to one hundred dollars—whatever your contract states. ESCs can also cover engine components, air conditioning and heating, and the power train, depending on which option you choose.

Here's another example of how an ESC works: Let's say you bought a three-year-old car with 37,000 miles on it. When it was new, the car had a five-year/60,000-mile transferrable warranty on it. That means you still have two years/23,000 miles left. You have the option of adding an ESC so the warranty covers beyond two years/23,000 miles. Depending on what the dealership offers, you could add an ESC with 36,000, 48,000, or even 60,000 miles. If the car has 37,000 miles when you buy it and it's covered for another 23,000 miles under warranty, adding a 48,000 ESC means you are protected until the car reaches nearly 110,000 miles.

Most cars with 100,000-plus miles are usually sold as is because they have no remaining warranty from the manufacturer. If an ESC is available, the coverage will be limited. The combination of year and miles offered might also be different.

There's a reason why nearly every dealership in America has a service department attached to it. Cars break down, and when they do, it can be very costly—especially considering the way computers run cars these days. The exterior of a car hasn't changed much over the years, but the interior has changed tremendously. Figure 8.1 illustrates the complex wiring system in many of today's cars. According to one of my finance managers, there is more computer power in a car today than what guided *Apollo 11* to the moon!

Figure 8.1. Wiring system on a small SUV

GAP COVERAGE

When Heather purchased her car from Taylor Automotive, she chose not to purchase GAP (Guaranteed Asset Protection) coverage through the dealership. Instead, she bought it through her car insurance provider because she thought it was cheaper. Ten days after Heather bought her car, someone rear-ended her and totaled the car. When she called her insurance company about having GAP pay the difference, she discovered that policy only paid if the accident was her fault.

As a result, Heather was left with a balance of $6,175 and no vehicle to drive. Her advice: "Listen to your finance manager when they tell you the advantages of the products!" After her accident, Heather bought another car from Taylor, rolled the negative equity ($6,175) into her new loan, and bought GAP coverage through the dealership.

* * *

In December 2017, Julie traded in her 2006 Chrysler 300 for a 2013 Ford F-150 and rolled the negative equity into her new loan. Julie's finance manager showed her the benefits available to her, and she chose to buy GAP coverage.

In October of 2018, Julie totaled her F-150. Her insurance company valued the vehicle at $14,200, and Julie still owed thousands more than the vehicle was worth. The GAP coverage paid the difference, including her $1,000 deductible. The GAP coverage also paid off the remaining balance on her loan. Julie was able to buy a new car with no negative equity and probably cut her monthly payment in half.

* * *

Kay purchased a new 2017 Kia Optima and financed $32,000 with payments of $610 a month. Almost exactly one year later, she was in a bad accident. Luckily no one was hurt, but Kay's Optima was totaled.

Because she paid attention when her finance manager shared the protection options available to her, Kay purchased GAP coverage for $700. Her insurance company paid the actual cash value of $13,900, which left a loan payoff of $12,708. The GAP coverage paid off the amount owed, and Kay was able to get a new Optima without carrying over a balance from her previous loan.

GAP stands for Guaranteed Asset Protection. This coverage protects customers in a situation where their car is totaled and they still owe money on the car. GAP coverage would pay the remaining balance between the actual cash value of the car at the time of the accident and what the customer owed.

GAP coverage may be added when you purchase and finance the vehicle. You can buy it through the dealership or through your insurance company. Either way, make sure you find out what is covered. As Heather found out the hard way, GAP coverage through your insurance company usually covers at-fault accidents only. Some GAP policies cover up to the original purchase price, but no more. That means if you add negative equity from a previous balance into the current loan, that additional amount probably wouldn't be covered. In Julie's case, she had GAP that covered both the current loan and the remaining negative equity.

As mentioned earlier, the cost of repairs has gone up over

the years, mainly because of the computers and electronics in cars, but even deployed air bags have become too expensive to replace. Because of the high price of repairs, insurance companies are much quicker to declare a car totaled after an accident, rather than trying to repair it. This is another reason to consider GAP coverage.

Accidents happen. For as little as ten to twenty dollars a month, you could potentially save yourself thousands of dollars if you get into an accident and total your car.

TIRE AND WHEEL PROTECTION

Juan purchased his 2016 Hyundai Elantra from Taylor Automotive and bought Tire and Wheel Protection as part of his package. In 2019, Juan hit a curb and blew out his front tire. He came in to have it fixed under the plan, but he didn't think he would get the tire replaced because the incident was his fault. He was even happier when he was told there was no deductible. New tire at no cost!

* * *

Monique purchased a car from Taylor Automotive. When she came in for an oil change, she advised the service department that one of her tires seemed to be losing air. When service was complete, she was surprised that she owed no money. She had forgotten she'd purchased the Tire and Wheel

Protection. Her oil change and tire repair (due to a nail she unknowingly picked up) were all covered.

* * *

When Barbara bought her 2013 Chrysler Town and Country, she purchased Tire and Wheel Protection and financed it through her loan, increasing her payment by less than ten dollars a month. Four months after she purchased the vehicle, Barbara hit a curb and needed a new tire. The coverage paid for a new tire, and Barbara didn't have to pay up front and then wait to be reimbursed. She simply brought her car back to the dealership and drove away with a new tire.

Also referred to as Road Hazard Protection, this product provides coverage to your tires and wheels. It protects you if your car sustains damage from potholes, chuckholes, nails, debris, flat tires, and blowouts. In some policies, it also covers your tires should you hit a curb.

A few years ago, I could have used this coverage. A new Kia Stinger had recently arrived at the dealership, and I had taken the car home for the weekend to test it out. On the way to my son's basketball game, I hit two huge potholes. I bent two rims and ended up with two flat tires. I had to pay for it to the tune of $1,800.

For five to ten dollars a month, you could save yourself an $1,800 bill like this.

OTHER PRODUCTS

Extended Service Contracts, GAP coverage, and Tire and Wheel Protection are the three most common ancillary products, but there are others:

- Paint and Fabric Protection covers the exterior and interior of your vehicle. A clear coat is applied to the exterior, and it protects the paint from things like acid rain, industrial fallout, bird poop, and bugs. Inside, a Scotch-guard type product is applied to the upholstery, making it a lot easier to clean up food and drink stains.
- Credit Life Insurance is a life insurance policy that pays off the loan if the buyer (or co-buyer if joint coverage is purchased) passes away.

TAYLOR TIP

Don't automatically say no when the finance or business manager at the dealership asks you about adding ancillary products. Remember the stories in this chapter and listen to the options for protecting your investment.

There are options out there to help you save money, but you have to be willing to listen to how they benefit you. Don't be closed-minded when it comes to these products. You may have always said no because that's what you were taught or because it's become a reflex reaction. Like the happy customers highlighted in this chapter, you might be so thankful one day that you spent a little extra to protect your investment.

CONCLUSION

What is the future of car buying? Is the day coming when dealerships will disappear and people will buy cars online the way they buy shoes or clothes? I don't think so.

According to the National Automobile Dealers Association's 2019 midyear report, over 16,700 new US dealerships started in the first half of 2019.[3] This tells me that even though Americans love buying things at the click of a mouse, they still want to go to a brick-and-mortar store when they buy a car. They want to sit in the driver's seat, grip the steering wheel, smell that new car smell, and take a test drive. They want to talk to someone face-to-face about their color choices, their trade-in's value, and their finance options. While the internet is an excellent tool for doing research up front, it can't replace the personal touch of a dealership.

Although car-buying won't shift to the internet, the World Wide Web has changed the way people buy cars. Facebook, Google, Yelp, and other social media have forced dealerships to become more focused on customer experience. If a potential buyer can search hundreds of dealerships in minutes, dealerships have to find a way to stand out. The key is how they treat their customers.

CUSTOMER EXPERIENCE

One of our customers had saved money for a down payment on a new car, only to have a family member steal the cash. She was a single mom with a sick child, and she needed to drive her child to Cleveland for doctor's appointments. We tried to get her a car loan, but we couldn't get her approved, partly because she didn't have money for the down payment.

The salesman who worked with this woman felt so bad for her. He told another salesman what had happened. That salesman had just bought a new car and was in the process of selling his older Honda. "Hey, why don't we just give her my car?" he asked. "She needs it more than I do."

The salesman who was working with the woman paid to have the Honda completely checked out in our service department—brakes, oil, tires, everything—and then they gave her the car.

The woman was so grateful. She shared a post online, which was picked up by the news, who came in to interview the two salesmen. These guys did what they did because they're good guys. They did it for no other reason than they thought this person needed help and they wanted to help.

That's the personal touch you won't find if you buy a car online. That's the kind of dealership you want to do business with.

You have a choice.

You should enjoy your car-buying experience. You should feel comfortable about bringing your car there for service. You should feel like family, confident that the dealership is going to take care of you if the car has issues. You should have no hesitation about sending family and friends there and about going back when you need a new car or you want to buy one for your teenager. If these things aren't true, find another dealership.

Many people think of buying a car as a necessary but dreaded transaction. Part of the dread comes from the uncertainty and the fear of getting ripped off. If you can find a dealership that treats you right and gives you a fantastic customer experience, your dread and uncertainty will disappear.

ACTION PLAN

My hope is that after reading this book, you feel you are on a more level playing field. I hope you feel you can walk into a dealership with confidence because you've gained some knowledge and practical skills. I also hope you now see car salespeople as allies who want to guide you through the process, not enemies who are trying to swindle you.

Here's a simple plan to take what you've learned and put it into action:

1. Before you do anything, check your credit score. Try websites like Credit Karma or FreeCreditScore.com.
2. Determine your budget. How much can you realistically afford for a monthly car payment? Try the simple math trick from chapter 3.
3. Research cars. Part of this process will be narrowing down type (SUV, sedan), manufacturer, and whether new or used will best fit your budget and lifestyle. I suggest narrowing it down to two or three cars. The guidelines in chapters 4 and 5 can help.
4. Research dealerships. Consider the points outlined in chapter 2: look at dealer websites and Facebook pages, check reviews and testimonials on multiple sites, and look for a dealership that seems to care about more than the bottom line. Don't forget to visit several so you can get a sense of the culture and level of service.
5. Buy a car! With information on negotiating, trade-ins,

and products to protect your investment, you have the tools to walk into a dealership and buy a car. And remember to be nice. This goes a long way in establishing that long-term relationship.

Car buying doesn't have to be a stressful or miserable experience. It can seem overwhelming because there are so many moving parts, but if you do your research and come prepared, you can make an educated and informed decision and walk away feeling happy about your purchase, while also saving time and money. That's the Taylor Made way to buy a car. Have fun!

ABOUT THE AUTHOR

STEVE TAYLOR owns and operates seven of northwestern Ohio's leading car dealerships, including the previous number-one-selling Kia dealership in the country. An eight-time winner of the prestigious Kia President's Club, Taylor Kia has also been honored with the International Kia Dealer of the Year award.

A recipient of the Outstanding Corporate Philanthropist Award, the Better Business Bureau Torch Award for business ethics, and the 20 Under 40 distinction from Leadership Toledo, Steve has also been a finalist for the Jefferson Award in public service. Steve calls Perrysburg, Ohio, home with his lovely bride of more than twenty years and their three wonderful children.

NOTES

1   Source of numbers in figure 3.3: Yowana Wamala, "Average Auto
    Loan Interest Rates: 2020 Facts and Figures," ValuePenguin,
    updated April 13, 2020, https://www.valuepenguin.com/
    auto-loans/average-auto-loan-interest-rates.

2   National Automobile Dealers Association, *NADA Data 2019:
    Annual Financial Profile of America's Franchised New-Car
    Dealerships: Midyear Report*, https://www.nada.org/WorkArea/
    DownloadAsset.aspx?id=21474855962.

3   National Automobile Dealers Association, *NADA Data 2019*.